THE SEVEN
DEADLY SINS

AND

THE SEVEN
CARDINAL VIRTUES

REV. JAMES STALKER, D.D.

THE SEVEN
DEADLY SINS

AND

THE SEVEN
CARDINAL
VIRTUES

JAMES STALKER

AMERICAN
Tract Society

NAVPRESS
BRINGING TRUTH TO LIFE
NavPress Publishing Group
P.O. Box 35001, Colorado Springs, Colorado 80935

The Navigators is an international Christian organization. Our mission is to reach, disciple, and equip people to know Christ and to make Him known through successive generations. We envision multitudes of diverse people in the United States and every other nation who have a passionate love for Christ, live a lifestyle of sharing Christ's love, and multiply spiritual laborers among those without Christ.

NavPress is the publishing ministry of The Navigators. NavPress publications help believers learn biblical truth and apply what they learn to their lives and ministries. Our mission is to stimulate spiritual formation among our readers.

CONTENTS

PREFACE

Originally published as two separate volumes in 1901 and 1902, *The Seven Deadly Sins and the Seven Cardinal Virtues* is just as applicable to readers today as it was to believers almost one hundred years ago. The seven deadly sins serve as warnings to those following Christ along the path of life—for it is these sins and those that stem from them that often lead us astray. In the same way, the acts of cultivating the seven cardinal virtues build Christlike character and lead to a life that is pleasing to God.

Although some editing has been done to update certain words or clarify the author's meaning, the original message of this book is essentially intact. At times the style of *The Seven Deadly Sins and Seven Cardinal Virtues* may seem quaint to today's reader. Readers will also note that the views Christians in that era held regarding the Christian life, church, and social issues may seem very different from commonly held perspectives. In addition, most Bible passages have been changed to that of the *New International Version*.

The Seven Deadly Sins and *The Seven Cardinal Virtues* were originally published by the American Tract Society. Founded in 1825, the American Tract Society was at one time the largest publisher of both Christian and secular titles in the world. During the 1800s and early 1900s, the society published works by many well-known authors and theologians, including John Bunyan and Jonathan Edwards. The American Tract Society also published biographies, devotionals, reference works, books of theology, and children's books.

In the 1940s, they stopped publishing books and focused exclusively on tracts—pocket-sized pamphlets. Most of their current tracts emphasize evangelism for all occasions on a variety of contemporary subjects and social issues. The American Tract Society is one of the largest producers of gospel tracts in the world today, publishing between twenty-five and thirty million each year. A free full-color tract catalog is available by calling (800) 54-TRACT or (972) 276-9408. For further information about the background and current ministry of the American Tract Society, write P.O. Box 462008, Garland, TX 75046 or visit its web site at http://www.gospelcom.net/ats

NavPress and the American Tract Society have an exclusive publishing relationship in which NavPress will republish selected works from the American Tract Society book archives that address classic spirituality, family, and Puritan theology.

AUTHOR'S NOTE

THE SEVEN DEADLY SINS

As the subject of this book may, by its novelty in Protestant religious literature, attract the attention of preachers desirous of leading their flocks to fresh fields and pastures new, it may be mentioned that its history, as a theological topic, is given in Zöckler's *Das Lehrstück von den Sieben Hauptsünden*, and that each of the seven sins is discussed with great acuteness and comprehensiveness in Aquinas's *Summa (Secunda Secundae)*. The order varies in different writers; I have adopted that of the scholastic catchword SALIGIA, composed of the initial letters of the words *Superbia, Avaritia, Luxuria, Invidia, Gula, Ira, Accidia*.

JAMES STALKER
Glasgow, March 1901

THE SEVEN CARDINAL VIRTUES

In case any of my brother-ministers should think of discoursing on the subject of this book, a word or two may

9

be prefixed on the literature. The whole moral system of Aquinas's (*Secunda Secundae* of the *Summa*) is built on this framework; and a marvelous structure it is, well worthy of the attention of all who wish either to sharpen their logical faculty or to widen their view of the moral world. On the heathen virtues an admirable discussion, thoroughly up to date, will be found in Mezes's *Ethics*, and on the Christian ones a discussion still more profound in Harless's *Christian Ethics*. Something on nearly every one of the topics discussed in the following pages will be found in any of the numerous works on Christian ethics, such as those of Schleiermacher, Rothe, Martensen, Dorner, Köslin, Newman Smyth, and Strong.

JAMES STALKER
Aberdeen, September 1902

PART 1

THE SEVEN DEADLY SINS

THE SEVEN DEADLY SINS

In war it is a great advantage to possess a thorough knowledge of the country. Soldiers fighting on their own ground are able to attack when not expected, draw the enemy into ambushes, and vanish when hard pressed without paying the penalty of defeat. It is of equal importance to possess accurate information as to the numbers of the opposing side, their strength in the different arms, and their material equipment. The lack of such knowledge may involve, even for the victors, an enormous expenditure of life and treasure. These rules are no less true of spiritual than of physical warfare. If we are to cope with the tempter, we must not be ignorant of Satan's devices, and we must know the nature and the extent of the forces which he brings into the field. For this reason it has been one of the tasks of theology to enumerate the sins that beset the human soul, to search into their subtlety, and to expose their methods of attack; and, as the result of many centuries of observation, seven sins have been especially noted as the leaders and chieftains of those that war against the soul—pride, avarice, luxury, envy, appetite, anger, and sloth.

These seven sins are nowhere all mentioned together in any single passage of Scripture, although, of course, they are all often mentioned separately. It is open to anyone to question whether there are not others entitled to the bad pre-eminence of being called the deadly sins, but the selection of these for this position is a conclusion reached, after centuries of discussion, by some of the acutest intellects of the race. I may refer in subsequent chapters to the history of the process by which this conclusion has been reached, but in the meantime I invite my readers to the study of the sin which heads the list—pride.

✦PRIDE✦

It may not seem obvious that pride is the primary sin, but this has been the pretty unanimous conclusion of those who have investigated the subject most deeply; and it will reward anyone to think about the reasons why they have come to this conclusion. It will be remembered that this was the first sin of which we have any knowledge, for it was through pride that the angels fell; and the outstanding feature of the character of the leader of the angels in that tragic drama, as Milton has depicted it, is arrogance. "Better," he cries, "to reign in hell than serve in heaven." In like manner, the sin of our first parents, which brought woe to all their descendants, was pride; the tempter whispered to them, "You will be like God" (Genesis 3:5). Besides, upon reflection, you will perceive that in no other sin is the very essence of all sin so concentrated. The essence of sin is selfishness, and pride is the inordinate assertion of self; it would annihilate others, and it disdains to be prescribed to even by God.

The Latin name for pride, *superbia*, means aiming at what is above, and Chaucer says that proud is the one who will always be aiming high. But the mere desire of what is above us is not pride. Not to desire what is above us would be not to desire any kind of improvement. Those, indeed, who aim at excellence will always be exposed to the charge of pride, but the accusation may be groundless. A learned person cannot help being aware of knowing many things which an ignorant person does not; and by the latter it may be supposed that the learned person must be proud on this account; but the increase of knowledge may, on the contrary, make one more humble every day. In promiscuous company, if a woman refuses to join in an uncomely game, she will be reproached as proud; however, her maidenly modesty is really beautiful and virtuous. It is impossible to display any constancy or zeal in religion without being accused of pride, as if you consider yourself better than others. There are those who call anyone who will not join them in riot and excess a Pharisee and a hypocrite, but God Himself has said, "Come out from them and be separate" (2 Corinthians 6:17). There is such a thing as proper pride; and, when an accusation of pride is brought, the accuser requires judgment as well as the accused.

In pride, there is always an element of falsehood. It is a claim to merits not possessed; or, if we possess them at all, we deceive ourselves and attempt to deceive others about the degree to which we possess them. We deny and ignore the claims of others, in order that our own may be pre-eminent. We hate those who estimate us exactly for what we are worth; and arrogance, in its extreme manifestations, demands that everyone suspend judgment and accept its self-estimate at the point of the sword. This falseness seems to me to be the distinctive mark of pride.

✠ ✠ ✠

Many kinds of pride have been distinguished. There is, for example, pride within, in the heart, and pride without, in the clothing, the furniture, or the like; however, as Chaucer characteristically remarks, the latter betrays the existence of the former, as the wine in a tankard at the door of a tavern speaks of the wine that is in the cellar.

Pride may be in thought, in speech, or in action. On speech it has an extraordinary effect. There are people whose conversation is nearly all about themselves. As often as the conversation strays to other subjects, they bring it back, for whatever the subject, it reminds them of something that has happened to themselves, and this immediately becomes the absorbing topic. They know how to bring the conversation round by the most circuitous routes, in order to return to this favorite topic. They think their devices are unnoticed, but everyone perceives them, for pride is constantly overleaping itself. It tries to make self out to be great and, in the very act of so doing, proves it to be little. It is no uncommon thing for a person to be laboring to convince people of his or her superiority, when transparent vanity is, in fact, making that person the laughingstock of the whole company. Boastfulness easily leads to exaggeration and exaggeration to falsehood. It is no uncommon infirmity to be unable to speak the truth about ourselves. Everything that has happened to us must be wonderful, and everything we have done must be great. And, as we puff ourselves out, people are saying behind our backs, "You cannot believe a word that person says."

The most fruitful division, however, of the different kinds of pride is, in my opinion, that founded on the different kinds of gifts by which it may be excited. These may be gifts either of nature, fortune, or grace.

Among the *gifts of nature*, intellectual talents are often accompanied by an inflated sense of importance with the craving for recognition and notoriety. The person of moderate gifts believes himself a nonesuch, and she who has achieved a little fame considers the applause of her coterie the murmur of the world. A Roman satirist spoke of "the irritable race of poets," but all those with an artistic temperament have an itch for recognition and applause which, unless it is held in restraint by good feeling and good sense, makes them discontented with the acknowledgment they receive and disposed to believe that the praise they deserve is being withheld by their enemies. In a character like the German philosopher Nietzche, this self-importance is seen grown to such colossal dimensions that he makes out of his own morbid cravings a philosophy of existence, teaching that the only law for us is to grasp the universe in our desires and then march forward to realize our ambition, in utter disregard of the happiness of other people. This is the epitome of pride.

Perhaps it is among women that the temptation is strongest to be proud of the gifts of the outward person, as it is chiefly on them that nature has bestowed beauty. It is not wrong to give to the body a certain degree of attention or to be happy in the possession of a fair face, but "charm is deceptive, and beauty is fleeting" (Proverbs 31:30) if it hides from its possessor the value of the soul or hardens the heart to the claims of others. It is not wrong to dress with care, but pride comes in when the attempt is made to appear to be something you're not. In

these days, when athletics are so much in vogue, it is, perhaps, rash to say that the temptation to pride in the body
is stronger in the one sex than the other; for, I fancy,
there must be an enormous development of vanity in
connection with the exhibitions of strength of muscle and
fleetness of foot before the crowds that gather to witness
athletic contests, and with the reporting of these in the
newspapers. On the other hand, the judgments of a crowd
are uncompromisingly exact, and we are brought to our
senses when we have to measure our strength and skill
against competitors. Learning the precise truth about ourselves tends to produce a humble mind.

The *gifts of fortune* are most dangerous when they
are given suddenly and unexpectedly. The Bible is full of
warning to those who have been exalted to prosperity, lest
they should become proud and forget to whom they owe
their wealth: "Jeshurun grew fat and kicked; filled with
food, he became heavy and sleek. He abandoned the God
who made him and rejected the Rock his Savior"
(Deuteronomy 32:15). It is not only, however, in the Bible
that this tendency is noted. In the satiric literature of
every age the sauciness and extravagance of those who
have risen rapidly to opulence are objects of attack. Few
have the steadiness of head and hand to carry a full cup,
especially if it has been suddenly filled. The upstart for-
gets old friends, is ashamed of poor relations, and is an
abject flatterer of those wealthier to gain even more. Seldom is the sin of pride witnessed in more repulsive forms
than in the vulgar ostentation of the *nouveaux riches*.

Even *spiritual gifts* may be a cause of pride. Even

humility itself may give occasion to it, and one poet makes
pride say:

> I am that voice which is the faint,
> First, far-off sin within the saint,
> When of his humbleness he first
> Takes thought; and I become that thirst
> Which makes him drunken with his own
> Humbleness, and so casts him down
> From the last painful stair that waits
> His triumphing feet at heaven's gates.*

The typical instance of pride in spiritual gifts is the
Pharisee, on whom our Lord Himself pours the vials of
His sacred scorn. When we speak of sin, it is nearly always
of the sins of the publican, the sinner, and the harlot. But
Jesus, while casting a cloak of charity over the transgres-
sions of these classes, mercilessly exposed the pride of the
Pharisee and the scribe. To Him pride appeared to be the
master sin.

The Pharisee must have been, to some extent, consciously a pretender. He concealed the secret sins for
which he deserved the contempt of others, and he wore
a pretentious garb of virtues to secure the homage of the
ignorant. But, for the most part, he deceived himself as
well as the public. He believed in the reality and trustworthiness of his own righteousness and boldly chal-
lenged the verdict not only of others but of God. And

*Arthur Symons, "The Seven Sins" in *Images of Good and Evil*.

herein lies the fatal danger of spiritual pride: *it renders spiritual progress impossible*. The Pharisee does not know that he is a bad man; how, then, can he be made a good one? If he knew, he might repent and betake himself to the source of spiritual strength. But God cannot save a person who is not aware of the need for salvation. This is the main reason why pride is so often denounced in the Bible and placed by the wise first in the list of the sins. It is the deadly enemy of salvation. Salvation is the grand work of God, but a humble mind is required to appreciate and seek it. The publican who casts his eyes on the ground and beats upon his breast, groaning, "God, have mercy on me, a sinner" (Luke 18:13), is an empty vessel, ready to receive the gifts of redeeming love; but for a Pharisee, satisfied with himself and with nothing to pray about but his own merits, what can even redeeming love do? Pride frustrates the grace of God; it stays the hand of mercy; for the proud the Savior has died in vain.

✛ ✛ ✛

If any of the old books on the seven deadly sins are opened, it will be found that, after speaking of a sin in its causes and manifestations, they always finish with the remedies for it. What, then, are the remedies for pride?

Anything that makes us think more of God or of our neighbor is a remedy because, as I have said, the essence of pride is selfishness. We are proud because we are thinking of ourselves alone and have forgotten the claims of God and the claims of our fellow creatures. We have forgotten that God has given us all our gifts, whether of nature, fortune, or grace. These belong to Him; we are only stewards of them, and there is a day coming when we shall have to give an account of how they have been employed. And, if we receive our gifts that we may be the stewards of God, we also receive them to minister to others. It is only a false greatness which lords it over others; the golden greatness consists in service.

In Dante's *Divine Comedy* those denizens of Purgatory* who are being cleansed from the sin of pride are represented as walking over a marble path on which, like the words or figures on a flat tombstone, are carved pictures of notable historical instances of humility. By looking on these they are unlearning their arrogance. We need not wait for the next world, or any fancied scene of purification there, to put this into practice. Look at a figure like Moses in the Old Testament, who was "more humble than anyone else on the face of the earth" (Numbers 12:3); or the Virgin Mary in the New, coming with her humble offering of two pigeons to the altar of the Lord; or look at John Knox, fleeing to hide himself when called upon to preach for the first time; or the late Dr. Cairns, whose friends discovered only after he was dead that he had been offered the principalship of Edinburgh University—look on men and women like these and learn how poor and false is the glare in which pride makes gifts to shine, in comparison with the gracious light with

---

*The scheme of the "Purgatory" follows the order of the seven deadly sins.

which they are invested by humility. But look, above all, to Him who said, "I am gentle and humble in heart" (Matthew 11:29). His entire history is one continuous lesson of humility; for "though he was rich, yet for your sakes he became poor, so that you through his poverty might become rich" (2 Corinthians 8:9). Who can stand beside His cradle and still be proud? Who can stand beside the Carpenter of Nazareth and still be proud? Who can stand beside the Friend of publicans and sinners and still be proud? Who can stand beside the cross and still be proud? "This is how we know what love is: Jesus Christ laid down his life for us. And we ought to lay down our lives for our brothers" (1 John 3:16).

⚜AVARICE⚜

No one who has pondered much on the course of human life will be astonished at avarice holding a high place on the roll of the deadly sins, for it has played a conspicuous and an evil part in history. The old authors who wrote on the seven deadly sins used to assign to each of them a number of offspring—that is, of sins which each breeds— and the offspring assigned to avarice were numerous and ill-favored. A large proportion of the wrongs and crimes of history has been due to the inordinate greed of gain. Indeed, the Bible itself says that "the love of money is the root of all evil" (1 Timothy 6:10, KJV). Many attempts have been made to soften this statement. Attention has, for example, been drawn to the fact that it is not about money the statement is made, but about the *love* of money. Then, it has been pointed out, the correct translation may be "is *a* root of all evil," not "*the* root." Evil has many roots, and this is one of them. Or, again, the meaning may be that every kind of evil at one time or another springs from this root—it may spring from other roots here or there, but somewhere it is always springing from the love of money. In spite, however, of these ingenious sugges- tions, I am persuaded that the text means what it says. It is a magnificent hyperbole, to denote how widespread is the evil which money does—corroding the hearts of people, spoiling their happiness, and setting them in con- flict with one another. "Man's inhumanity to man makes countless thousands mourn"; but the inhumanity springs, for the most part, from the desire of one person to possess that which belongs to another.

The lust of one country for the soil of another has, thousands of times, let loose war and pillage on innocent populations. The powerful have, in every age, under the sway of similar motives, plundered the goods and oppressed the weak. The lawful hire of toilers has been kept back by their employers, and human law has been too servile to say no; and so the rich have filled their granaries with the food which ought to have fed the poor, and worn purple and fine linen that ought to have covered the naked. The love of money has begotten the courage of the highwayman; it has sharpened the ingenuity of the thief; it has, many a time, put a knife in the hand of the murderer; and for thirty pieces of silver Judas sold his Master.

But, besides such tragic crimes, the record of which reddens the pages of history, what a progeny of sordid sins the love of money is bringing forth every day. It teaches merchants to adulterate their goods, employees to steal from their employers, lawyers to lie, operators on the stock exchange to swindle their clients. A Latin satirist, twenty centuries ago, charged the Roman fathers of his day with saying to their sons, "Get money; honestly, if you can; but, in any case, get money." A satirist of our own age alleges that, in modern life, the only unpardonable sin is poverty. On every hand people are making haste to be rich, and, if they succeed, everything is forgiven them. The gates of highest society swing open to those who have gold, and they are not asked how they came by it. Over those who have swindled and failed, society, with upturned eyes, pronounces an annihilating judgment. The adventurers who bring home bullion tinged with the blood of slaves are welcomed as an honor to their country and sent into Parliament.

One of the offspring of avarice that the old writers used to mention was *gambling*, and the need has not gone by for indicating the true place to which this vice belongs. The desire to make money is undoubtedly at the bottom of the practice—to make money in haste, without giving any equivalent for it—and this is its condemnation. But, after it has grown into a habit, it becomes a very complex thing. The gambler can hardly tell why he or she follows with such eagerness the events of the green turf and the fortunes of the green table. There is a fever in their blood which drives them on, rendering ordinary pursuits and ordinary gains stale, and making their own hearts reckless and hardened. A single act of gambling has an innocent look, and the first steps in a gambling career are frequently exhilarating; but the atmosphere soon becomes grimy, the associations and companionships into which it leads are demoralizing, and many a time it ends in jail.

Such are the offspring of avarice, and the character of the progeny does not say much for that of the parent. What the innermost nature of avarice is may be learned from the well-known words of Scripture—"Greed, which is idolatry" (Colossians 3:5). Pride, the first of the deadly sins, is also a kind of idolatry: it is putting self in the place of God. But avarice substitutes for God an even more amazing deity—something outside of ourselves, earthly and material. We think with disdain of the folly of the heathen, who bend the knee to graven images; but many have money for a god, and the coins of silver and of gold that they finger so caressingly are in reality images in which their deity is embodied. This may seem a figure of rhetoric, but it is the sober truth. For, what is it to have a god? It is to have an object to which the heart turns with supreme affection and to which the mind looks as a refuge and defense in all the changes and chances of time. Are there not those who feel the money they possess to be a far safer assurance against possible calamity than faith or prayer, and those who would feel the loss of the opportunities of worshiping God afforded by the Sabbath and the sanctuary a far less sensible calamity than the loss of their money?

This unconscious idolatry sits deep in many hearts in the form of what our Lord called "carefulness"—that is, a lifelong dread of poverty, a sense that, not having money, they have no protection and no hope. For avarice is not confined to those who are wealthy: the poor may be equally the victims of it. Excessive elation in the possession of money and excessive depression on account of the absence of it are, in fact, the same feeling—that money is the true divinity, beside which there is no other. It is no unusual thing to hear the avarice of the rich denounced in a spirit of the most sordid greed, the language betraying the belief that money can do everything and making it patent to the critical hearer that the orators, if they possessed money, would be as absorbed in it and as forgetful of the claims of others as those they denounce. The one who is loudest in denouncing tyrants often becomes a tyrant when the chance is presented; and those who cry out for equality are sometimes the first, when they have obtained the upper hand, to shake off the claims of fraternity. The worship of money is not a religion which favors the brotherhood of humankind.

Deep students of human nature have spoken of avarice as incurable. Thus Dante, personifying it, says,

> Accurst be thou,
> Inveterate wolf, whose gorge ingluts more prey
> Than every beast beside, yet is not filled,
> So bottomless thy maw.

Many, at the beginning of their career, dream of no greater fortune than a few hundreds; but, if they are successful, that which was once the limit of their ambition soon becomes only the starting point. They may have been humble and prayerful and thankful for their early successes, but, as money carries them further and further away from the habits and associations of youth, their hearts harden, and their faith is transferred from God to Mammon; they become proud of themselves and contemptuous of others. Thus the very goodness of God makes them forgetful of their Maker. As long as they were little, they recognized the hand from which their mercies were received, but—sad perversion—when mercies are multiplied, the Giver is forgotten.

Avarice affects us all but is distinctively a sin of the old; and it is this which makes the cure of it so hopeless. As other sources of happiness fail, this one seems to grow more substantial and the flattery, which the dependent are too apt to bestow on those from whom they have expectations, produces by degrees a sense of omnipotence. On the canvas of the painter a miser is usually represented as an old man clutching with thin and bony fingers a bag of gold. But this is a fancy picture. The real danger, which has to be resisted by old and young alike, is the tendency to believe that, if we have money to trust in, we can dispense with both the blessing of God and the sympathy of others.

I have not hesitated to paint this deadly sin in its true colors, but I should feel that I had rendered to my readers a very indifferent service, if I merely left on their minds the impression that money is an enemy of which they must beware. Everyone knows better, and nothing tends more to associate the pulpit with unreality than sermons which leave impressions of this kind. Everyone knows, on the contrary, that money is a good thing; most people are giving the sweat of their brow and the force of their brain for it; they are well aware that without it they cannot set up a home and fill it with refinement; families and countries that are exercising the virtues of industry, honesty, and sobriety tend to grow rich; and art, science, and even religion are, in many ways, dependent on money. The fact is, young people are in quite as much danger of putting too little value on money as too much. They often fling it away with both hands, to their own injury and that of others. Extravagance is nearly as much the besetting sin of youth as avarice is the besetting sin of age; but virtue lies between the extremes, and its name is liberality.

To be forearmed against avarice we require to have three convictions sunk deeply in our minds.

The first is that *there are better things than money*. Good health is better; a cultivated intelligence is better; a sympathetic heart is better; a clear conscience is better. With these it is possible to be happy without money; but without these the happiness which money gives is deceitful. Not only, however, must these be prized, but so diligently acquired as to prove that their possessor knows he or she cannot do without them. A cultivated mind, for example, that knows something of the best thoughts of the best thinkers of the past, or an active sympathy with the wants and aspirations of humankind, is not obtained by merely wishing but by working honestly and feeling deeply; only, when it is once got, it cannot be parted with, for it is felt to be a possession beyond all price. I know a public man in a great position who was approached, when the election was hanging in the balance, by the representatives of a party in the electing body who wished him to make a promise to them which would have secured their votes. His answer was, "Gentlemen, there are some things in this world I can do without, and one of these is this office for which I have been named; but there are some things I cannot do without, and one of these is my honor—good day, gentlemen," and he bowed them to the door. This is the attitude we should take up to the temptations of avarice. There are some things we can do without, and one of these is wealth. However, there are some things we cannot do without, such as a clean conscience and a useful life, and, if we must choose between money and these, we forego the money.

A second conviction, to be engraved still more deeply on the mind which would defend itself from the invasions of the sin of avarice, is that *money is not an end in itself, but only a means to an end*. It will tyrannize over us if it is allowed, but we tyrannize over it, and prove ourselves its masters, when we compel it to serve the ends that we have freely chosen as our own and which our judgment and conscience approve.

When anyone has much wealth, we are wont to call him "a person of means." But not infrequently the phrase is a misnomer because means imply ends to which they are devoted, and many a wealthy person has no such ends. He does not know why he makes money; he is like a horse turning a mill, accustomed to the monotonous round; he is the slave of money, which claims all his thoughts and all his energy. Yet the phrase "a person of means" conveys the hint that money can be used in promoting rational and useful ends, and this is true. People often speculate on what they would do with money if they had an immense amount of it. Such musings may not be amiss, but they are mere illusions, unless we are devoting to the same ends such means as we now happen to possess. David Livingstone, before he thought of being a missionary, devoted to foreign missions all his wages as a patternmaker, except so much as was required for his frugal personal wants. One wonders that this should not be more common. But multitudes who have never felt called upon to sacrifice all their income in this way give liberally of their earnings to causes that lie near their hearts, and they experience a profound satisfaction in so doing because they feel that they are making their money serve their life aims, and they are keeping themselves free from enslavement to it. I remember hearing a friend tell of the effect on himself of his first givings to his church. He was not earning much at the time, and what he gave cost a real effort and sacrifice but he felt that he now had something to work for. This heightened his consciousness as a man and a Christian; it made him look so carefully after his money that, he maintained, he was a gainer, even monetarily, in the long run. Giving is usually spoken of as if it were the wringing of unwilling drops out of flinty hearts; but there is a remarkable verse in the account of the gifts offered in David's time for the temple that Solomon subsequently built—"The people rejoiced at the willing response of their leaders, for they had given freely and wholeheartedly to the LORD. David the king also rejoiced greatly" (1 Chronicles 29:9). There is great joy in giving, when it is not forced and indiscriminate but willing and intelligent—that is, when we give to causes with which we are well acquainted and for which we cherish enthusiasm. Ought it not to put new energy into our fingers and help us to sing as we toil, when we reflect that we are earning money to assist the cause for which the Savior died?

The third principle about money deserving to be inscribed on the mind that would escape the bondage of avarice is that *it cannot be kept forever*. "Do not store up for yourselves treasures on earth, where moth and rust destroy, and where thieves break in and steal. But store up for yourselves treasures in heaven, where moth and rust do not destroy, and where thieves do not break in and steal. For where your treasure is, there your heart will be also" (Matthew 6:19-21). There are those who mock at such teaching, declaring the idea of a treasure in heaven to be merely an illusion by which the poor are blinded to the treasure which is their due on earth. A paradise above the skies is only an invention of priests to cheat people out of the paradise they ought to seek here below. If this be so, how sad it is that the earthly paradise lasts so short a time even for those who attain it. The existence of heaven may be doubted, but there is no denying the reality of death. However much you may have amassed, you have in a moment to leave it all and fare forth into the unknown, naked as you came from your mother's womb. What have you, then, if there is no Savior to meet you on the frontier of the other world and conduct you safely to the many mansions? Are you not poor indeed? But, if you have realized within yourself a virtuous and holy character, this is a possession over which time has no power; it is incorporated with your very existence, and you carry it with you wherever you go—even across the threshold of death. If you have spent your life doing good and making enemies of the mammon of unrighteousness, you will be met at the gates of heaven by grateful hearts, which have gone before and will welcome you into everlasting habitations. It may be said that the avaricious have at least the satisfaction of leaving their money to their heirs. But this is a mixed satisfaction for they do not know whether their heirs will be wise or foolish, whether they will keep what they have inherited or squander it. The influence, on the contrary, of a benevolent and useful life goes on after death and reproduces itself in those whom it awakens to aspiration and imitation.

> Only the actions of the just
> Smell sweet and blossom in the dust.

⚜LUXURY⚜

The Latin name given by the old writers to the third of the seven deadly sins is *luxuria*, and I have translated it literally by the English word "luxury." But our word is a euphemism for what was meant, for the sin which the scholars thus designated was what we should rather call sensuality or licentiousness—in a word, all offenses of whatever kind against the seventh commandment, "You shall not commit adultery" (Exodus 20:14).

This is a sin of which it is difficult to speak, and in ordinary circumstances the less said about it the better. Silence is sometimes more eloquent than speech, and the reticence in which this sin is shrouded is the severest of all condemnations for it signifies that sins of this kind are so bad that it is a shame even to speak of them.

Still, reticence may be carried too far. The Bible is not silent on this subject. On the contrary, it not only speaks but thunders against it. In the book of Proverbs, for example, which is especially intended as a handbook of the journey of life, there is no other sin treated with so much amplitude and repetition. There is abundance of facts—of secrets known to all—in the life of the present day in both town and country to lay on the pulpit the obligation, unless it is to exhibit cowardice, to speak, if not frequently, at least firmly and fearlessly on this subject. Too absolute ignorance on the part of the young concerning the kind of world they are living in may give temptation a cruel advantage over them, for the force of temptation often lies in surprise. One of the things impressed on my mind by what I have come to know as a minister is the early age at which the most dangerous temptations have often to be faced. Even at school attempts may be made to corrupt the mind. Young men are certain to be tempted, the assault on their virtue sometimes coming from the most unlikely quarters. Young women need to be warned, as they go out into the world, that their ruin may be attempted by the very men from whom they should receive consideration and protection. No doubt there is a danger of kindling, by speech, the very fire we wish to quench; but there is an instinct in healthy minds that tells them whether what is said on this subject proceeds from pruriency or moral earnestness. I am not much afraid of being misunderstood, while I am sure that I can calculate upon sympathy in discharging a difficult duty.

Let us begin where the Bible begins—with our *thoughts*. Our Lord Himself said that "anyone who looks at a woman lustfully has already committed adultery with her in his heart" (Matthew 5:28); and St. Paul confesses that his own first sense of sin arose from the power of lustful thoughts. To such purely internal motions of the flesh heathenism attached no importance; and there are many to whom, so far from being repulsive, they form a part of the pleasure of existence, to which they return whenever their thoughts are released from occupation with other subjects. But there can be no doubt that these are of enormous importance to character. It is not only that the indulgence of such thoughts in secret prepares the way for open yielding to temptation, but such thoughts themselves deeply stain and pollute the soul. The more they are repeated, the more the mind returns to the same subject. Physiology would say that in the very substance of the brain, channels are dug to make the course of the current easy till, at last, control is wholly lost, and the brain becomes a pandemonium of licentious scenes and images. Even the life of dreams is invaded by the habit till, to a conscience not wholly blunted, sleep itself may become a kind of terror.

The true defense against this tyranny of a foul imagination is the preoccupation of the mind with healthy subjects. What is bad can be kept out only by filling the mind beforehand with what is good. The more numerous wholesome interests we have the better, to keep us from brooding on illegitimate themes. The mind depends to a considerable extent on the body, and a good state of health, kept up by plenty of exercise, fresh air, and cold water, is an effective foe of foul thoughts.

Secondly, this sin may be committed in *words*. In this respect, indeed, there has been a vast improvement in the habits of society. A hundred years ago, just as profanity in speech was notoriously prevalent, even in the highest classes, so there was a freedom in speaking of those things of which it is a shame to speak that would not now be tolerated; and, if you go further back in the history of this country—say, to the period immediately before the Reformation—you will find that our nation [Scotland] has been slowly emerging from a horrible pit of grossness. Open talk of this kind is now banished to the lowest and rudest portion of the population, and the one is branded who attempts to introduce it into society that has any respect for itself. Yet there are circumstances in which the old evil habit tends to return. For example, when young men meet together in the evening there is a tendency, as the night grows late, to allow the conversation to wander on forbidden ground. Then men reveal what is in them—the objects on which they brood and dream when they are by themselves—and one story of a questionable kind calls forth another. It is an hour to exercise watchfulness. A man who, in such circumstances, holds himself aloof will always command the respect of those whose approval is of value; and the silence of even one member of a company will not fail to touch the consciences of the rest, for all are in their hearts ashamed of the beast in themselves which they are permitting to become visible.

Along with conversation may be mentioned reading of an unhealthy character. This is a difficult subject because it is not easy to say where the line should be drawn and because this is a case where the maxim holds good, that what is one's food may be another's poison. A mind pure and mature may peruse with advantage books that would be to another like fire taken into the bosom. Young readers should not be ashamed to confess to themselves or, if necessary, to others that there are books which they cannot read with impunity; and, whatever be the course which others may pursue, they should judge by the effect produced on their own imagination.

In this respect also we are in a vastly improved position in comparison with our fathers. Last century the books in the English language adapted for hours of recreation and amusement were stained through and through with moral depravity, resembling, in this respect, the bulk of French literature at the present day, which, I often think, must reduce to despair those in that country who are really concerned about the morals of the young. It was the Evangelical Revival that drove the satyr from English literature, and it is only the prevalence of an earnest religious spirit that can keep it out. Ever and anon it attempts to show its cloven hoof, and there cannot be a doubt that there are pens ready enough, for the sake of gain, to minister, if they dared, to the vilest passions. But it is not possible to be thankful enough for the general tone of literature amongst us during the last hundred years — for great poets, like Wordsworth and Coleridge, Tennyson and Browning, who have uttered nothing base, and for great imaginative writers, like Scott, Thackeray, and Dickens, who are at this hour finding worthy successors in the writers of the Scottish school. In the work of all these there is presented an ideal of love, which has done an immense deal to refine the habits both of thought and action in the population. In the older writers love is confounded with lust, but these authors all recognize and teach that "lust is no more love than Etna's breath is summer, and love is no more lust than seraphs's songs are discord." There is, in fact, nothing which so successfully banishes lust from the thoughts as a pure and absorbing affection; and there are no better teachers than those who foster in the popular mind the belief that this passion is our chief earthly happiness. Our poets and novelists have constituted themselves a priesthood of the love of woman in a way not dissimilar to that in which preachers are the priests of the love of God; they make the attainment of this love the goal of life in the same way as ministers make the love of Christ our chief end; and, in fighting down the brute and cultivating the unselfish emotions, we owe much to the earthly as well as to the heavenly evangel.

On *deeds* of sensual sin—the third aspect of the subject— I naturally hesitate to say anything. The peculiarity of such sins is that they involve the guilt of more than one. And herein, to a mind which has caught any faintest breath of the spirit of Christ, ought to lie the strongest defense against committing them. To sin oneself is bad enough, but to involve another soul in sin is diabolical, and especially in sin which brings such utter shame and reprobation as this does. The complaint is often made that the punishment falls so much more severely on the one sinner than on the other, and it cannot be denied that the contrast is cruel; yet the loss to society would be infinitely greater than the gain to justice if the inequality were to be redressed by lowering the standard of womanly purity. Rather, the change must take place in the opposite direction—by causing man to feel how hideous a crime it is to sacrifice the character of another to his own desires. This he ought to feel out of his own heart, but, if he has not enough manliness to do so, it ought to be brought home to him by the aversion and stigma of society.

It is not, however, true, though one would fain believe it, that temptation invariably comes from the side of man. By taking this for granted, a young and inexperienced soul may find itself unexpectedly in a most dangerous position. This was the peril to which Joseph was exposed, and many in every generation since have been surprised from quarters as little suspected. Surely Satan never achieves a triumph more complete than when she who was intended by her Creator to be the priestess of chastity and to refine and elevate man's coarser nature becomes his temptress and lures him to his undoing; but the streets of every city in the world bear painful evidence to the success with which even this master stroke of hellish deceit has been achieved. In this respect some of our cities are honorably distinguished by the comparative decency of the streets, and too much credit cannot be given to the public officials to whom this is due; but in others open vice has been allowed to reach dimensions which are a horrible public scandal; and every young man going from the country to the town ought to be forewarned. There is no sin which more quickly or inevitably destroys soul, body, and fortune, and, especially to this open and unblushing form of indulgence, nature herself has attached penalties of disease, descending often from generation to generation, so ghastly as to act as a glaring danger signal on the downward road.

✣ ✣ ✣

Most of what I have said has been intended to put readers on their guard against being surprised by this sin, and I have taken it for granted that the conscience will immediately condemn it as soon as its true nature is realized. But not infrequently in the literature of the day there is insinuated a libertinism designed to corrupt the conscience, and many minds are subtle enough to invent for themselves the same kind of sophistry. If, it may be argued, this appetite is native to humans, why should it not be indulged like any other natural desire? This is an argument which often has been used to break down the defense of virtue.

But our appetites are not given us merely for indulgence but also for restraint. Each one has to be kept in its own place. If we surrendered ourselves, without restraint, to our natural impulses, we would be beasts. It is mastering our impulses, and the exercise of self-control, that sets us apart as human.

And this is the supreme instance in which self-control has to be exercised. Here the effort is more difficult, needs to be more frequently repeated, and is more prolonged than anywhere else. But the reward is correspondingly great. It is great in social life, for the chaste nation is the strong and prosperous nation; and what would the family be without chastity? It is great, too, for the individual:

> So dear to heaven is saintly chastity
> That, when a soul is found sincerely so,
> A thousand liveried angels lackey her,
> Driving far off each thing of sin and guilt,
> And, in clear dream and solemn vision,
> Tell her of things that no gross ear can hear.

Granted that the instinct is one of the very strongest in our nature, is it not worthy of the Author of nature to have consecrated it to the sole service of unselfish love? Fatherhood, motherhood, childhood, home—there are no more sacred words in the world than these; and that warmth is worthy of a unique consecration which, moving secretly in the stock of humanity, causes such exquisite flowers to burgeon on its surface. The Christian rules of chastity may seem harsh or cruel, but they are the prickly sheath which guards the most perfect flower of human happiness. A young man's worthiest dream is to see himself the center of a virtuous home, to which he has brought a purity as perfect as that which he demands in the partner of his life, thus ensuring, as far as in him lies, the health and character of those who may come after him. This is the true earthly paradise: it is worth toiling for, it is worth waiting for, and it is worth denying oneself for.

Yet this is not the highest motive. We cannot dispense with that old motive with which Joseph defended himself in the hour of temptation, "How then could I do such a wicked thing and sin against God" (Genesis 39:9). What the tempter whispers is, "No eye will see you, nobody will ever know"; there are circumstances in which this argument comes with terrific force, as for example, in a foreign country, where the stranger is not known to a single soul. But there is an Eye which sees everywhere. Blessed is the one who respects the conscience and God as much as a whole theater of spectators.

Even yet, however, we have not reached the final motive. There is no sin which holds its victims in more

hopeless captivity than this. If you have fallen under its
power in any form, it is almost impossible to escape again;
as the book of Proverbs says of the strange woman, "None
who go to her return or attain the paths of life" (2:19).
But the impossible is not impossible to God, for with God
all things are possible. Christ Jesus is the Savior not only
from guilt but from sin, and from this sin as well as others. Of this there is an immortal illustration in the case
of perhaps the greatest intellect ever won to the service
of the gospel.

St. Augustine was, in his unregenerate days, held cap-
tive by this sin, and in his *Confessions* he told the story
of his miserable bondage and his ultimate and complete
emancipation. At the crisis of his conversion, he was
plunged in horrible distress between the force of inclina-
tion on the one hand and the call of conscience on the
other, but it was a power far above his own that rescued
him at last. He was sitting in a garden with his companion, Alypius, when he suddenly rose to seek a lonely place
where he might give way, unobserved, to his emotion. As
he went, he heard a voice, as of a boy or girl playing,
which said, "Take and read, take and read." He turned
back, and, lifting a book which happened to be the Epis-
tle to the Romans from the table at which his companion
was still seated, he let his eye fall on the first words which
met him, and they were these: "Let us behave decently,
as in the daytime, not in orgies and drunkenness, not in
sexual immorality and debauchery, not in dissension and
jealousy" (Romans 13:13). These were God's own words,
and in them the hand of God gripped him. He felt that

the long struggle had been taken in hand by One mightier than himself. Christ had redeemed him and from that time forth, in union with Christ, he became a holy man. When Christ is in the heart, no sin can permanently abide in it. The love of Christ constrains us to abandon every thing inconsistent with His presence. "Do you not know that your body is a temple of the Holy Spirit, who is in you, whom you have received from God? You are not your own; you were bought at a price. Therefore honor God with your body" (1 Corinthians 6:19-20).

ENVY

Envy is grief or displeasure at the good of another—the good consisting of wealth or fame, or any other possession which people prize. And it is only the reverse side of the medal if we feel delight and exultation in another's evil— in failure or ill success, or any other kind of calamity.

It is of consequence in the case of this sin to be particular about the definition, because there are motions of the mind not unlike it that are not vicious but virtuous. There is, for instance, *emulation*, which is frequently confounded with envy, but is, in fact, quite different. Emulation is also excited by a neighbor's good; but the effect is not the same—envy produces a sense of depression and despair, but emulation produces feelings of admiration and imitation. Emulation may, indeed, desire to excel the virtue or ability which it copies—this is its nature—but it does so not for the sake of outstripping a rival, but in the sheer desire for excellence. Envy, in short, is ill-humored, and emulation is a good-humored desire to excel. The old writers used to distinguish from envy another feeling to which they gave the name of *nemesis*—a word which we do not now use in this sense; in fact, I hardly think we have any name for the feeling itself. It was lawful, they thought, to grieve over the success of another or to rejoice in his downfall, if it was in the interest of the public cause. Thus a good man might lawfully grieve over the social elevation of a neighbor whose influence was likely to lower the moral tone of the locality, or a patriot might lawfully rejoice in the downfall of a tyrant. Perhaps, also, we may lawfully grieve at others' worldly prosperity, if it is obviously doing them spiritual harm, and wish to see their career checked, to make them think. But such sentiments are easily corrupted by the introduction of a personal element because as one of La Rochefoucauld's biting maxims says, "Few are able to suppress in themselves a secret satisfaction at the misfortunes of their friends." At all events, it is the selfish element which is the poisonous ingredient in envy—the sense that we are affronted because another rises, or that we reap benefit and gratification from another's humiliation.

It may not be thought that this sin is worthy to be ranked with those we have already discussed—pride, avarice, and luxury—and certainly, in some respects, it comes short of their colossal proportions. But there is something extraordinarily mean in the spirit which is unhappy and disappointed because another succeeds, while it glories in another's misfortunes. Such sentiments betray a selfish isolation and an utter absence of love which cannot but be both demoralizing to character and, in the highest degree, displeasing to the God of love.

In history, envy has been the cause of some of the greatest crimes. The second notable sin of the world—the murder of Abel—was prompted by this base passion. Cain could not bear that there should be anyone more acceptable to God than himself. And may we not say that a great many of the persecutions and martyrdoms suffered by the people of God in every age have been due to the same cause—to the spite of the wicked at the existence of those whom they have secretly felt to be better than themselves?

A great many of the worst sins of the tongue are the product of envy. It is miserable to think how much of conversation consists of disparaging remarks about the character or the talents, the position or the conduct of others. Gossipers cannot but admit the brilliance or the benevolence of the person they are criticizing, but—oh, with how many of these envious "buts" is conversation garnished. Those who make use of them not infrequently claim for themselves, as they do so, the character of virtue: they are sorry they have to say what is about to follow, really it gives them pain to have to reveal it, but truth compels. Yet they have been working up to it all the time: they have only laid on the praise that they might the more effectively introduce the exception which was to cancel all. There are those who are cleverer still: they do not themselves make the damaging statements, but draw them out of the mouths of others, openly deprecating the censures in which they secretly rejoice.

How is it that we can be so petty and so false? Why should the humiliation of another thus afford us gratification? There are people who are sick with fear lest another should attain an honor which they themselves have not been able to reach and sick with chagrin because others are happier than themselves. But the worst element in their own unhappiness is their pettiness. Envy is its own punishment. To be consumed by this passion inwardly, and to live and move outwardly in an atmosphere of gossip and detraction, is a hell upon earth. Yet many are living in it.

Not only individuals, but families, classes, and even nations, can allow themselves to fall into this state of mind. There is a widespread belief that the glory and prosperity of our own country [Scotland] are regarded by certain other countries with chronic envy. However, this idea is probably exaggerated and, at all events, it will be safer for ourselves to remember that other nations believe us to be chronically the prey of a feeling not dissimilar to envy — the desire of Ahab for Naboth's vineyard (see 1 Kings 21). There is that bitter feeling between rich and poor which, on the part of the less fortunate, is mere envy of the more fortunate. On the Continent this has been a prominent feature of the propaganda of socialism and communism. I have myself sat an entire day in a gathering of the International, where orators from the great cities of Germany were haranguing a crowd of working men. From the oratorical point of view, the speeches were of the most brilliant quality, but not one word was said of the interest or pride which one should take in work for its own sake, the only string harped upon being denunciation of the plutocracy for running away with more than its own share of the spoil. In the contests among ourselves between the different classes of society there has hitherto, I think, prevailed much more of the spirit of good-humor. And long may this continue; for nothing can poison the happiness of any class so completely as envy for the goods of those above them. By all means let emulation prevail, and let the pathways be opened to merit; Also, it would do no good to those underneath in the social scale to blot out the image of a more refined life displayed in the class above them; for this is the very magnet which draws them upwards.

There are, no doubt, some natures more inclined to the sin of envy than others. It has sometimes been spoken of as a sin of the strong, who cannot endure that smaller people than themselves should appropriate any of their praise or obtain any share of their possessions; and there have been in history remarkable instances of this insane desire to engross everything, as, for instance, that of Alexander the Great, who is said not to have tolerated any praise of his own generals, esteeming any recognition bestowed on them as subtracted from his own glory. But, I should fancy, envy is principally a vice of the weak, who, finding themselves beaten in the competition of life, grow sick with disappointment and are ready not only to envy others but to reproach God. "Why has He created me as I am?" "Why has He not given me the gifts lavished on others?" As well might anyone ask, "Why am I not six feet high?" As well might the clay say to the potter, "Why have you made me this way?"

Very moderate abilities may be associated with limitless ambitions. A woman with but a tolerable voice may be as hungry for praise as a *prima donna*, or the orator of a town council covet as much recognition as would be the due of a statesman able to command the applause of listening senates; and, when the expected tribute is not paid, the sensitive, artistic nature is plunged in gloom and discontentment. Not infrequently envy is the fruit of idleness and laziness. Many have been endowed by nature with talents sufficient to win for them a foremost place, but they have not made use of them. Instead of living laborious days, they have expected fortune to drop into their lap, and, instead of cultivating their minds by burning the midnight oil, they have calculated on winning the prize by genius or cleverness alone. Then, when they see the object of their ambition passing to those who have worked for it, they murmur against Providence and blame their stars. But they have only themselves to blame. A man of distinction, who was being assailed by envious detractors, said, "They wish to have my fortune, but why do they not wish to have my labors?"

If it be asked how envy is to be cured in a nature which may be prone to it, I should say, first of all, *Learn to love excellence for its own sake*. In an old castle in the heart of Germany, celebrated for its picturesque situation and its noble proportions, and rendered famous by the fact that Martin Luther spent one of the most eventful years of his life in it, there is a wonderful series of proverbs painted on the walls, one of which runs as follows:

I love a thing that's fine
Ev'n when it is not mine,
And, though it never mine can be,
Yet it delights and gladdens me.

For many a year this old rhyme has haunted my memory and helped me, I hope, to keep envy at bay. To have an eye for whatever is fine, even though it is not ours and never can be ours, immensely increases our resources, for the world abounds with fine and noble things, and in a real sense they belong to us if we have the power of appreciating them. I once said to the owner of an estate in which I had the privilege of walking, and in which I walked nearly every day for years, that it was more mine than his, for he seldom visited it; and we may become very rich if we make the most of all the fine things that are accessible to our observation and enjoyment.

This argument acquires far more force when those whom we are tempted to envy are using their talents for the glory of God and the good of the world. What! Do we grudge that humanity should be served and God glorified by powers superior to our own? Would we impoverish the cause of progress or of the gospel by restricting it to the support of those inferior to ourselves? We cannot love the good cause very passionately if we do not welcome every talent consecrated to its service. Yet, it is to be feared, envy enters sometimes into the most sacred service. The human nature in a minister is tried when someone settles in the same town whose fame puts out the light of his popularity, and it may take a time before even a good man can say, "He must increase, but I must decrease." There is a kind of vicarious envy which it is even more difficult to check—when our family or friends are more jealous of our position and influence than we are ourselves, and find it more difficult than we to brook the interference of a rival. Thus, in the Old Testament, the family of Moses looked with an evil eye on the prophesying of Eldad and Medad. But the great man of God, rising above the sentiments of his own champions, said to Joshua, "Are you jealous for my sake? I wish that all the LORD's people were prophets and that the LORD would put his Spirit on them" (Numbers 11:29).

In like manner, when St. Paul's friends were drawing his attention to the shortcomings of rival preachers, he said, "But what does it matter? The important thing is that in every way, whether from false motives or true, Christ is preached. And because of this I rejoice. Yes, and I will continue to rejoice" (Philippians 1:18).

I will give you one more remedy for envy: *Count your mercies*. The envious are always comparing themselves with their more fortunate neighbors; but the world contains many who are less fortunate than any of us; and why should we not sometimes think of them? If you ever enter an almshouse or a poorhouse, you will feel yourself to be wealthy, even if you have only a moderate income; if you pass through the wards of a hospital, you will thank God for your good health, even if you sometimes have a headache or a toothache; and so, by thinking sometimes of the multitudes less gifted or less prosperous than ourselves, we shall make the springs of gratitude flow within us. Do the mercies we have to be thankful for include the great salvation? Is our soul redeemed, and do we carry the hope of immortality in our breasts? If so, how can we ever be disappointed or envious? If we only realized how much we possess when we possess Christ, our mouths would be filled with laughter and our tongues with praise all the day long, and, catching the spirit of the Savior, we should be able to rejoice with those who rejoice and to weep with those who weep; this is the final victory over envy.

⚜APPETITE⚜

There are three appetites which inhere in the flesh of humans—the appetite of hunger, the appetite of thirst, and the appetite of sex. Of the third of these I do not require to speak here, having treated it fully in the chapter on luxury, but the other two call for attention in the present chapter.

Appetite, being part of the apparatus of the human constitution, has, of course, an important part to play in the economy of life; and it is not its use, but its abuse, which is sinful.

Hunger is one of the sternest facts of human experience. The appetite asserts itself every day and has to be satisfied. The time and strength of the great majority of the human species have to be expended in providing food for hungry mouths, and the task has to be discharged on pain of death. The daily lighting of the culinary fire, the varied labors of the farm, the trades of the miller, the baker, and the cook, the transit of the products of different districts and different countries by means of the ship and the railway train and other conveyances—these, and a hundred other operations in which the services of millions of men and women are employed, are all concerned with satisfying the appetite of hunger. In fact, hunger may, without much exaggeration, be called the mainspring of the whole machine of human existence; for what else is it that sets people every day in motion and makes them acquire the arts and crafts by which they earn their daily bread? The appetite of thirst is even more imperative and requires to be satisfied at least as often as that of hunger. Happily, the means of satisfying this appetite are less costly, being liberally supplied by the bounty of Providence. Yet, in the complicated civilization of modern times, enormous and costly engineering operations have to be undertaken to supply water to large cities.

It is only what was to be expected, when we consider the loving Providence by which our life is arranged, that the satisfaction of the appetites is accompanied with pleasure. The honest discharge of daily work causes hunger to be felt at the right time, and, as the proverb says, hunger is the best sauce. It is when no work is done to produce hunger that much artificial seasoning of food is required to excite an appetite. It seems reasonable to believe that the satisfaction of the appetite of thirst is also intended to be accompanied with pleasure. How far the simple means provided by nature may be manipulated with this in view, as food is rendered more palatable by cooking, is a question by no means easy to answer in every case. At any rate, people, in all ages and in all continents, have made use of other substances besides water, such as the juice of the grape, to quench thirst, or they have fortified water with other ingredients to make the act of drinking minister to pleasure.

✣ ✣ ✣

It is of the abuse of these functions I have to speak today. And, first, the abuse of eating is the sin of *gluttony*.

Savages, whose supply of food is meager and uncertain, fill themselves to repletion when they get a chance, disposing at a single meal of a quantity of food which fills civilized onlookers with astonishment. The half-savage civilization of imperial Rome was distinguished by occasional carnivals of gluttony, the details of which, supplied by historians and satirists, inspire the modern reader with perplexity and disgust. In the moral treatises of the Middle Ages, very specific directions are given for avoiding gluttony, and it is manifest that this must have been a besetting sin of the monastic life. Inside the cloister there was too little variety to break the monotony of existence, and the dinner hour naturally became for many of the monks the most exciting of the day. They are warned, accordingly, against a number of sins which can be committed in eating — such as eating before the appointed hour, being too nice about the materials of food, indulging in too highly-spiced cookery, eating too much at a meal, and the like. All these precepts need to be enforced on children still, and, no doubt, there are adults also who would be the better of hearing them repeated. But, on the whole, I should be inclined to say that gluttony is a sin which the civilized person has outgrown; and there is not much need for referring to it in the pulpit. Physicians may occasionally give their well-to-do patients a homily on a simpler life or exhort their poorer patients to substitute cheap but substantial articles of food for the unthrifty and unhealthy diet they often make use of. However, such weaknesses hardly come within range of the dread artillery of the pulpit. It is a curious fact that a sin which was once an urgent topic in the teaching of morality should now be so rare that we can practically neglect it. Let us hope it is a sign that humanity is gradually leaving the beast behind and rising into habits worthy of themselves.

Unfortunately, if this can be truly said of gluttony, it cannot be said of the corresponding sin of *drunkenness*. While humanity has been acquiring control of the appetite of hunger, we have apparently been losing it as regards the appetite of thirst.

Every single act of drunkenness is a sin. It is a defacement of the divine image, a temporary dethronement of the power within us which ought to govern, and a casting of our crown of glory in the dust. Look at drunken people—helpless, mindless, unclean—and say if they have not sinned against their own humanity and against the Creator of the same. One of the worst features of drunkenness is that, when coming out of the intoxicated state, the drunk never believes that he has sunk so low as he really has, but, if he could see himself as others see him, he would have to confess how far he had fallen beneath the dignity of his being.

The sin of drunkenness is aggravated by the fact that it leads to other sins. It deprives the intoxicated person of self-control, and so gives the beast within free scope. What control has an intoxicated person over his or her own chastity? What control of temper? A cruel or even a murderous blow can be struck without the knowledge of what is done. There is not a day but the newspapers contain such incidents, which would in any other circumstances, make the blood of readers run cold, but receive hardly passing notice because they arise from this cause. The act of drunkenness grows by degrees into a habit, although the victim is generally unaware of what is taking place and is still quite confident of the power to manage the self long after the fiber of the will is completely relaxed. The whole moral nature, indeed, is slowly destroyed. First to go is the virtue of truthfulness for the slaves of this vice will say or do anything to obtain what they need to satisfy the appetite, and you cannot believe a word that a drunkard says. One after another all other fine qualities disappear; and these are sometimes very fine indeed for the victims of this vice are frequently the most gifted in both head and heart. Nothing is spared, until the end comes. It is said that sixty thousand die in this manner in these islands [British Isles] every year. What a procession of woe! Yet it is hardly noticed, it is so common. If it were the loss of a great war, it would sound, in notes of lamentation and woe, through the land in all the organs of public opinion, but it is only the nation's annual tribute to its favorite vice. What a hopeless procession it is, as it files into the eternal world for these poor men and women are going to appear at the judgment seat of Him who has said that we are not even to associate with drunkards (1 Corinthians 5:11).

Only half the truth, however, is told when we try to realize the sin and the misery of drunkards themselves. The evil spreads on every hand. Perhaps there is no drunkard who does not infect others with the same vice, for it is a conspicuously social sin. Besides this, however, multitudes suffer from it through no fault of their own. The drunkard's home is a proverb for misery and hopelessness. His wife is kept in a state of unceasing suspense and fear, which no language can describe, and the more refined and sensitive she is, the keener is her suffering. His children share the same feelings of humiliation and terror and their health is often permanently injured because the money which ought to be spent on their food and clothing is consumed on his vice. There are tens of thousands of children in our land growing up without a fair chance on this account. For it is not only here and there, at wide intervals, that this evil is doing its destructive work—it is everywhere. There is hardly a family in the country into the circle of which the pain and disgrace have not penetrated.

In short, this is the national sin at the present time, and it is making our country the byword of the world and drawing into itself, like a chronic sore, the force which should be invigorating every part of the body politic. The money, for instance, which should be spent on food and clothing, lodging and furniture, and which should be making the business of the baker, the butcher, the grocer, the joiner, and the mason to flourish, is poured into the insatiable throat of this appetite, doing nobody any good. A large proportion of the crime of the country has been attributed to drink by our foremost judges; and to the same cause must be referred most of the outlay of the nation on the expensive establishments requisite for dealing with crime and poverty.

In writing a lecture recently on the tragedies of Shake-speare, I was struck with the frequency of the references to this subject. Lady Macbeth confesses that she prepared herself for crime by taking stimulants. Of the drugged guards of the sleeping king, she says:

> That which hath made them drunk hath made me
> bold,
> What hath quenched them hath given me fire.

In *Othello* one of the characters says:

> I have very poor and unhappy brains for drinking;
> I could well wish courtesy would invent some
> other custom of entertainment.

And again:

> O God! that men should put an enemy in their
> mouths to steal away their brains. . . . O thou
> invisible spirit of wine, if thou hast no name to be
> known by, let me call thee devil.

In *Hamlet* the hero says of Denmark what many think about this country:

> This heavy-headed revel, east and west,
> Makes us traduced, and taxed of other nations:
> They clepe us drunkards, and with swinish phrase
> Soil our addition; and, indeed, it takes

From our achievements, though performed at
          height,
The pith and marrow of our attribute.

The magnitude and difficulty of this problem are mani-
fested by the numbers of the solutions attempted.

There are those who pledge themselves not to take
intoxicants except at meals, and not to treat others to it.
There is a great difference between taking drink as part
of food and taking it by itself, and there can be no doubt
that treating is one of the worst features of social life. A
publican has told me that five or six working men will
come into his shop on Saturday on their way home. One
of them treats the whole company, another does the
same, and so on it goes, till all have treated all, and all are
intoxicated. He told me, he could remember when the
same practice prevailed among gentlemen at the lunch-
eon bar; but in that class it had now, he said, entirely
ceased—each asks and pays for what he himself requires,
and then departs. And it was my informant's opinion that
the same change among working men would make a
world of difference.

It has often surprised me that no movement has been
set on foot to change the intoxicating liquors which are
drunk. No one who has traveled much on the Continent
can have failed to notice how rare it is to see an intoxicated person on the streets. Yet there is probably more
drinking in Germany or France than in this country. The
difference is due to the liquors consumed. If our working

class confined their potations to something as light as German beer, and the wealthier classes theirs to light wines, there would hardly exist a drinking problem. But it is by the strong and fiery intoxicants used by our population that the country is being ruined; and few are aware that it is within comparatively recent times that the use of these distilled spirits has become general.

In all probability, the next great step of reform will be a curtailment of the traffic by the interposition of the legislature. There is, indeed, an old and much-worn proverb which says that you cannot make people sober by act of parliament. But we are going to try the experiment, and that on a large scale. On this the country has made up its mind. Politicians of all parties have been very shy of approaching this question, but it overtops all their reforms. And of this the public mind is becoming so convinced that they will not be able much longer to give it the go-by. I hope the time is at hand when we shall see the rival parties competing with one another as to which is to be the executant of the will of the sovereign people; unless, indeed—which would be better still—God raise up a statesman of first-class power who will make this the absorbing object of his life.

There is truth, nevertheless, in the saying that you cannot make people sober by an act of parliament. Merely to shut the door of the public-house in the face of people who wish to go in is a very imperfect cure. How much better it would be if they did not want to go in, and consequently the door had to be shut from the inside. Why are people so eager to drink? There must be a vast, dull misery in their hearts to make them willing to sacrifice their means, their character, and their hopes for the sake of securing a temporary oblivion of their condition. Everything that imparts to men and women self-respect, that makes home more attractive, that interests them in their work, that gives them a future and a hope, is an enemy to drunkenness; and such positive counteractives must be brought into operation, as well as measures of repression.

But by far the most powerful reform of recent times has been the temperance movement, whose advocates consider the crisis so acute and the temptations so abounding, that, for themselves and their families, they judge it safest and best to abstain altogether.

This movement is not, as is often insinuated, one for personal protection alone. It is inspired still more by a patriotic and humanitarian spirit. Its adherents feel so keenly the disgrace of the country, the debasement of human nature, the suffering of families, the loss of immortal souls, that they are not satisfied with shielding themselves from attack but have pledged themselves to attack and to overcome this evil; they believe they can fight it best in temperance armor. Many of them would not admit that they are making any sacrifice because they consider life to be healthier and happier without the use of alcohol. Others feel that there is a considerable sacrifice in having to act counter to the habits of the society to which they belong, but they are willing to accept any sacrifice rather than be neutral in a cause in which the welfare of others and the glory of God are so directly concerned.

As to each and all of these modes of avoiding and opposing drunkenness, it is for everyone to be fully persuaded in his or her own mind; but it will always be the duty of the pulpit to insist on four things, not as matters of opinion, but in the name of God—firstly that *drunkenness is a deadly sin*; secondly, that *we are not to associate with drunkards*; thirdly, that *it is the vocation of Christians to use the most effective means for putting an end to everything that is dishonoring to God*; and fourthly, that *the only perfect defense against drunkenness is a living, working, and rejoicing religion*; as the Apostle says, well knowing why he places the two states in opposition to each other, "Do not get drunk on wine, which leads to debauchery. Instead, be filled with the Spirit" (Ephesians 5:18).

⚜ANGER⚜

Anger is a sudden heating of the blood, which flushes the face with color, while it makes speech forcible and action swift and sure. It is, in fact, a kind of military equipment, provided by nature to repel wrong and to avenge injustice.

It is not in itself sinful. There is a verse of Scripture which says, "In your anger do not sin" (Ephesians 4:26), and this implies that there is an anger which, so far from being wrong, is a duty. Many times in Scripture we read of the "wrath of God," and we read also of "the wrath of the Lamb." In the life story of Jesus we read that on one occasion He looked round on a certain company "in anger . . . deeply distressed at their stubborn hearts"; and what an image of indignant scorn He presented when He overturned the tables of the moneychangers and, with a scourge of small cords, drove the buyers and sellers out of the temple!

Such instances of holy indignation suggest what the legitimate use of anger is. It is an upboiling of resentment against unrighteousness, either to prevent it from happening or to antagonize it and sweep it out of existence when it has obtained a footing in the world. How natural it is we may learn from the well-known precept to fathers— "Do not exasperate your children" (Ephesians 6:4). Parents may act toward their children in such a way as to outrage the sense of justice in their hearts and make them feel that they are betrayed and injured by those from whom they are entitled to expect protection. It is not good for children that this force of indignant resistance to what is unreasonable should be broken in them, and it is not good for the mature. We may become too tame. As in a highly bred horse, however docile it may be, there always slumbers its native temper, so the excellence of human character depends on a sensitiveness of honor latent beneath the outward aspect of civility. To be utterly blind to insult and injury is not the evidence of a superior but an inferior being. Especially when the wrong is a public and impersonal one, it may be a sign of the debased state of moral feeling not to be roused by it to indignation.

So far from it being wrong thus to glow with anger at public unrighteousness, it is a sin to be tame and silent. The other day I was reading a series of articles by a strong young American thinker on "The Christian of the Twentieth Century," and, among other things, this passage occurred:

> There will be more and more need of great hatreds. Our talk of charity and tolerance must not blind us to the call for bitterness and wrath against all unrighteousness and ungodliness. The Christian of the Twentieth Century will know how to feel contempt as well as admiration, and detestation as well as love. It is related of Joshua Leavitt that once he greeted an advocate of the free love abomination, who came to see him, with the words, "Sir, I abhor you, I abhor you, I abhor you." "Do not I hate them which hate Thee?" asks

David, and he replies, "Yea, I hate them with perfect hatred." It was wrong to hate them as persons, but it would have been wrong to do other than hate their hatred of God. Soft and easy toleration of everything will be called by the honest names of treason and dishonor. No feeling of love for the pure can long survive a decadence of the feeling of hatred for the impure.

It was right to show that there is a legitimate and even an imperative indignation, but our chief business in this chapter is with the anger that is a deadly sin.

It is such when it is directed against wrong objects. The legitimate objects of anger are injustice and folly, but it may be provoked by the opposite objects. A man may, for instance, go into a towering passion because a religious friend displays anxiety about his soul. A son may sulk or even run away from home because of a reproof or a punishment thoroughly deserved. The thief is angry because his victim claims his own, and the tyrant because his subjects assert their rights. Pride and selfishness make demands that are thoroughly unjust, and wax angry with everyone who does not concede them. Our sense of our own merits and rights is generally far in excess of our sense of the corresponding claims of others, and hence arises strife. Anger in one disputant breeds anger in the other; this, again, reacts on the first offender; and so it goes on till great sin is the result. It is no unusual thing in a prolonged quarrel to find that people have forgotten what at the first it was about. It was a triviality, but the injuries entailed by the contention arising out of it may be the reverse of trivial.

Anger becomes sinful by excess. Even when there is a real cause for it, the outbreak may be out of all proportion to the offense. "Do not let the sun go down while you are still angry" (Ephesians 4:26) is a precept of both the Old Testament and the New and it would be well if this ordinance of nature—the setting of the sun—were universally agreed upon, wherever the sun rises and sets, as a signal to make anger to terminate. Jeremy Taylor narrates that Leontius Patricius was one day extremely and unreasonably angry with John, the patriarch of Alexandria. At evening the patriarch sent a servant to him with this message, "Sir, the sun is set," upon which Patricius reflecting, and the grace of God making the impression deep, he threw away his anger and became wholly subject to the counsel of the patriarch. The very same indignation which may be useful in its first outbreak becomes poisonous if allowed to sour into the vinegar of hatred and revenge; and it is not less dangerous to the heart in which it is entertained than to the person against whom it is directed. Few more troublesome guests can harbor in a person's heart than an angry and vengeful spirit.

Anger becomes sinful when it vents itself in ways that are unlawful. It is, for example, one of the principal causes of profane language. Of this sin it is the custom of the world to speak lightly, as if an oath or two here or there did not signify. But no one who knows anything of the love of God can think without horror of the name which angels adore being mixed up with the filth and dregs of our angry passions; and, therefore, those who revere the name of the Father and the Savior will avoid the occasions on which it is apt to be used profanely. It is not only, however, in words that anger vents itself, but in acts, and these are apt to be violent and excessive. An angry man may inflict a blow that fills himself with horror as soon as the deed has been committed. It may even be a mortal blow for he has so lost control of himself that his frenzy may carry him to any extreme. "Anyone who is angry with his brother will be subject to judgment" (Matthew 5:22) says the Scripture; he has surrendered himself to a passion, and he does not know how far it may carry him. Many a murderer who has expiated his crime on the scaffold has hated his victim less than the man of colder blood may hate his enemy while yet sparing to strike; however, the deeper the hatred, the greater is the crime in the eyes of God.

The form of anger which has most to be guarded against is temper. This is a chronic disposition to anger. Perhaps some have more of a natural tendency this way than others, but it is very general. How many people will confess that they are naturally of a hot temper! But this is a poor excuse, for a swift temper is there to be controlled; and, if it is controlled, it becomes an ornament instead of a deformity to the character, imparting an elasticity and spring to action, which is otherwise too sluggish. But a hot temper uncontrolled becomes a curse in the home. There are no bounds to the violence some allow themselves, and all about them have to suffer from their strident voices, ill-natured looks, and unjust actions. A person with a temper can keep a whole household in continual hot water. Still more intolerable are those who shut themselves up in sulky reticence, brooding over imaginary injuries, while the other members of the household do not know how to approach them or get a civil word out of their mouth.

Anger is, in short, the special sin of the home, and, therefore, it is specially odious to Him who has set us in families and intends the family to be the nursery of love and peace. A young man may be preparing for himself, and for those who will have the strongest of all claims on his affection, years of bitterness and sorrow by failing to chasten his temper before the responsibilities of married life begin; whereas a successful effort at self-control, maintained in early years, will ensure a lifetime of happiness to both him and his.

Many cures for the sin of anger have been suggested.

Children are often told that, if they could see themselves when angry—the sworn veins, the bloodshot eyes, the distorted features—they would never again allow themselves to become so ugly. And this is a lesson which the oldest of us may remember with advantage in a slightly altered form: anger is a triumph of the lower nature over the higher—a triumph of the beast over the angel. When temper is allowed to have its way, we are reverting to the savage. In the Middle Ages the aid of art was resorted to sometimes in order to impress the truth about the seven deadly sins; and anger was represented as a figure riding on a camel, the most vicious of all animals, while on the shield which it carried was painted a mad dog.*

Anger is a brief madness, but we advance along the sunny pathway of our own maturing when we leave anger behind and cultivate thoughts of helpfulness and charity.

All have heard the practical rule to count to twenty before speaking when angry; and, joking apart, any device or practice which allows the first few moments of anger to pass without an explosion is of the utmost utility because the second wave of angry emotion is much less lofty and crested than the first. Sometimes, when an angry quarrel is imminent, it is a good thing to walk off, to be out of harm's way; and it may shame an angry opponent if one is seen thus to avoid the triumph of unreason. Richard Baxter suggests that it is good to tell the person we are with when we feel the access of angry passion coming on; and certainly there are hours of inexplicable moody humor when we know beforehand that we are dangerous but have enough reason and good nature to be able thus to give warning against ourselves.

St. Augustine, writing to a friend, the Bishop Auxilius, counseled him, when the winds and waves of angry passion rush down on his soul, to do what the disciples did

*On the artistic representation of the deadly sins, see the book of Zöckler mentioned in the Author's Note.

in the boat when the tempest descended on them—call to Christ. If we could stay to interpose a quick prayer between the first fiery sensation of anger and its expression in word or deed, we should not often fall into sin of this kind, and our self-control would be still further confirmed by the frequent contemplation of Him who, "when they hurled their insults at him, he did not retaliate; when he suffered, he made no threats. Instead, he entrusted himself to him who judges justly" (1 Peter 2:23).

There are many people who had hot and violent tempers in early youth but now exhibit a calm and even disposition; and the change is due to many struggles, many humiliations, many prayers; for it is by such means, as a rule, that the victory is gained. But it seems to be possible, at a single step, to leave the angry habits of a lifetime behind and enter at once into the placidity and sweetness of the Christian temper. One may get such a sight of how displeasing a bad temper is to God, and how unworthy of a follower of Christ, that all at once the violent or morose mood will be slipped off, like a filthy garment, and the Christlike spirit put on. Of this I came across a remarkable illustration in a book I was reading the other day—the life of the Reverend George H. C. Macgregor, a well-known Presbyterian minister in London. His biographer, a gentleman of good sense and studied moderation, in describing a spiritual crisis through which he passed, says:

One striking effect was very soon discernible, of a kind which may well be recorded, because it is fitted to afford encouragement and hope to others.

Nature had given him a peculiarly high-strung nervous temperament. This was specially seen from his childhood in sudden paroxysms of temper, in which he would quiver from head to foot or fling himself passionately on the floor. Even when he grew up, these appear to have sometimes recurred. It was one of those things which, because they have to some extent a physical basis, even good men sometimes almost acquiesce in. One has heard a bad temper spoken of as a trial or a cross, as if it were, like lameness, a thing to regret, but beyond one's control or power to alter, to be accepted as a permanent fact of a human personality. That it is a cross, indeed, every Christian man cursed with such a disposition sadly knows. The struggle against it is often deeply discouraging; sometimes the only hope seems to be that it will mellow and soften somewhat as life advances. It was at Keswick that Mr. Macgregor first learned to think differently about this. There he learned first of all, as never before, to understand that yielding to any evil tendency, no matter how rooted in one's nature, were it hereditary twenty times over, is sin. It was in that season of self-examination and soul abasement when, as he wrote, "I have been searched through and through, and bared and exposed and scorched by God's searching Spirit," he had a special sense of the evil, and made a special agonizing confession to God of this besetting sin. And when, after these

days of consecration, he left Keswick, certainly, to
a large extent, the evil temper was left behind.
From that time, he was really, in this respect, a
different man. He would never have said, or
dreamed of saying, that his inward disposition was
all that it might be, or ought to be, absolutely con-
formed to the mind of Christ. Man's goodness is
always defective. Doubtless at times our friend was
ruffled. But there were no more paroxysms, and
those who knew him best knew how all but
unvaryingly serene his temper was.

SLOTH

Some of my readers may have felt a doubt now and then whether the sins traditionally recognized as the seven deadly sins are really the most dangerous to which we are exposed; and this feeling may be intensified when it is mentioned that the Latin name for the last of the seven is one for which it is difficult to find a simple and natural equivalent in modern speech. The Latin word is *accidia*. Chaucer attempted to naturalize this in English by calling the sin "accidie," and this winter I noticed in one of our religious periodicals a very able article headed "The Sin of Accidie"; but not one reader in a hundred would know, without explanation, to which sin the writer intended to point.

It has even been hinted that the sin itself is one of the past and has disappeared from the modern world. There can be no doubt that *accidia* held a more conspicuous place in the life of the monastic age, when the doctrine of the seven deadly sins was originally developed, than it does in modern life. "Those who are fasting about midday, when they begin to feel the want of food and to be oppressed with the heat of the sun, are most liable to the attacks of *accidia*," observes Thomas Aquinas, one of the great authorities of the pre-Reformation Church.

Accidia was defined as spiritual torpor—an aversion to religious exercises, which, on account of it, were discharged perhaps with mechanical regularity but without zeal or joy. It might sink by degrees into bitterness of soul and hatred of existence, and, if not counteracted, it might at last issue in lunacy or suicide. When we remember how many there must be among monks and nuns who have no real call to a life of contemplation, it is no wonder if a certain proportion of them live in a state of chronic disgust with their lot or fall into imbecility. Many readers will remember Gustave Dore's picture of "The Novice"—one of the most terrible transcripts from human life I have ever seen—a young man with the light of youth and genius in his face, introduced for the first time among those who are to be his lifelong associates in the monastery—a row of mindless, joyless figures, out of whom every spark of inspiration has long since died—and in the one terror-stricken glance he is casting over them may be seen the whole tragedy of his life as it must be in the future.

Religious exercises were never intended to absorb the whole of our time but to supply strength for the discharge of duty in the family and in the market-place; and the attempt to override nature cannot but have its revenge. The Roman Church condemns multitudes of men and women, intended by their Maker for social service, to spend their days in solitude, without the charities of home, without the presence of children, without the exhilaration of exertion; and the result must be, in many cases, untold agony and hopeless rebellion. No wonder that prayers incessantly repeated become meaningless, or that the soul, shut away from the healthy activities of existence, grows peevish and despairing. The sin, in such circumstances, is artificial; it is not so much due to the rebellious soul as to the tyranny of an evil system; and it is no wonder if human nature breaks down under a yoke it was never intended to carry.

There is no doubt that spiritual torpor and aversion to religious exercises are very real sins and so may be bitterness of soul and contempt of life; and these are the states of mind stigmatized by the term *accidia*.

In the end of the eighteenth and the beginning of the nineteenth centuries there was an outbreak in literature all over Europe called *Weltschmerz*—that is, disgust with the world, disgust with life, disgust with everything. It received its most famous expression in Goethe's youthful romance, *The Sorrows of Werther*, the hero of which, disappointed in love and despairing of happiness, shoots himself. An epidemic of suicide is said to have been caused by the popularity of the book. By putting his sorrows into words, Goethe cleared his own mind of the hypochondria by which it was beset. However, at the same time Lord Byron was, with less happy effect, putting similar sentiments into his poems, in which gloomy heroes rail against the laws of society and the customs of a world for which they deem themselves too lofty and noble. But, in reality, Byron was himself always the hero of his works, under a variety of disguises; and his savage contempt for society and for life itself was nothing by the weariness of a worn-out voluptuary. He had lost the taste for healthy pleasures and had so inured himself to unnatural ones, that at last he could get true satisfaction out of nothing and cursed the world because it could no longer supply anything to satisfy his hungry desires. The *Weltschmerz* of Goethe and Byron culminated in the pessimism of a Schopenhauer and Hartmann, by whom the nothingness of the world was stamped as a dogma and the existence of an overruling Providence denied.

There is a period in youth when a certain recoil from conventionality and a certain contempt for the world as it is may be anything but unhealthy for such feelings may be the seeds of progress. Young eyes see with astonishing clarity what is noble and what is base, what is right and what is wrong; they criticize without hesitation what offends their sense of justice. If they consecrate their energies to the task of remedying the evils they discern, great good may come of their noble discontent. But merely to criticize and do nothing cannot have a good influence. It sours the temper and produces a spirit of discontentment not only toward one's fellow creatures but even toward Providence itself. Especially as old age approaches, this spirit ought to be carefully guarded against. Many people, as they leave middle age behind, perceive that they have scored less highly than they had expected in the game of life, and yet their chance is past, never to return. Then comes the temptation to grow bitter against those who have been more successful and to refuse, because the great prize has been missed, to accept such opportunities as fortune may offer and to make the most of them. The sunshine fades from the landscape, and a gloom sets in which nothing can lift. "The Fathers of the Church often urge it with special emphasis, that a dejection and sorrow entirely absorbing a man is at bottom nothing but ungodliness, and proceeds from the devil, for it arises from unbelief in the gospel of Christ, and unthankfulness for the grace of God revealed in Christ."*

The inability to find any joy or satisfaction in the allotments of Providence is not, however, confined to those to whom the course of fortune has proved unkind; for the most utter weariness and disenchantment with existence will not infrequently be found in those who appear surrounded with every comfort or even luxury. I quote the following from the paper on "The Sin of Accidie," to which I alluded earlier:

> A large number of women in comfortable suburban homes are afflicted in this way. The necessaries, and many of the luxuries of life, are secured to them. Their husbands are in the city and their children at school; there is no immediate point of interest that appeals to them. Outwardly they might not unreasonably be expected to be thoroughly and unreservedly happy. And yet many a poor man's wife, who has to earn her living in addition to caring for her husband and children, is ten times as happy as the employer's wife, who has no such strain put upon her, but who, nevertheless, is profoundly miserable in the midst of her comforts—just because she has so little

*Martensen, *Ethics*.

demand made upon her energies. The remedy here is to find some channel of Christian and philanthropic work into which to throw the mind's energies and the heart's love. It is wonderful what a medicine for accidie is found in disinterested and hearty service for others. The fogs of melancholia vanish, and the inner sunshine returns, when we do something for another human being whom we can benefit. How many miserable women would be happy if once they tasted the joy of doing good.

"Sloth" is the term I have chosen, in the title of this chapter, for the old theological word *accidia*; and, although it is hardly wide enough to cover all that was intended, it has an extensive scope and is capable of bringing the sin home to our own consciences.

Spiritual sloth or torpor is exhibited on a vast scale by those classes of the community that entirely neglect the worship of God. These are often spoken of, under the name of the lapsed masses, as if their condition were their misfortune and not their fault. But they are all the creatures of God, living on His bounty. In a thousand ways they have experienced His goodness and mercy; many of them are daily receiving at His hand all things richly to enjoy—for the lapsed are not confined to the poor—and yet they give Him no thanks and take no pains to stir up their hearts to gratitude and praise but, on the contrary, keep Him as far as possible out of their knowledge. They are suppressing the most glorious powers of their own being, for undoubtedly the noblest part of our nature is that which links us with the divine. I like to see in the streets, on Sunday evenings, the groups around open-air preachers, for these are an evidence that even in the most careless and abandoned there exist chords that vibrate to the Word of God and the tones of worship. But the god-ward powers within us ought not to be left to such casual impulses; they need careful and constant culture, and the place to obtain this is the house of God.

Irregularity and carelessness on the part of those who are connected with the church are generally due to the same cause. Indeed, I am inclined to think that there is no greater enemy of the church than sloth. People who take on boarders have often complained to me of the way in which, on the Lord's Day, all the arrangements of the household are thrown into confusion by those who are not only prevented by their own sloth from being in the house of God but prevent others also from attending who would like to be present.

Yet the fault is not all on one side, for young people have complained to me that it was impossible for them to attend the Sabbath Morning Meeting because of the delay and lateness on Sabbath morning in their lodgings. Such malarrangements may appear to be trifles, but, if their effect be to stunt the growth of character at the critical stage, and thus to destroy the powers and influence of the whole subsequent life, it is manifest how serious they are. Nothing can be a trifle that interferes with the work of the Spirit of God.

I remember an intimate friend, when we were fellow-students together, after he had passed through a great spiritual crisis, saying to me, "I have been perishing through sheer sloth." What he meant was, that for years he had been quite well aware that it was his duty to be up and doing—acting on his convictions, confessing his Savior, and taking his share in God's work—but that he had procrastinated owing to a kind of torpor and unwillingness to be bothered. Does not his confession sum up the real history of many a soul?

There are times when a sort of spiritual numbness steals over the spirit. Prayer becomes remiss; the Scriptures become dry, and the reading of them a duty more than a pleasure; motives which have stirred us to the depths of our being appear no longer to act. In this condition evil habits come back and secure a footing in the places from which they have been dislodged; we begin to think we have been too puritanical in denying ourselves and breaking with the world, and we venture upon dubious paths on the plea that they cannot be demonstrated to be absolutely wrong. This is backsliding; and what does it consist of, when you examine it closely, but spiritual sloth?

The grand remedy for such a state of decay is to remember that the normal condition of a Christian is one of joy. Joy is not only an occasional privilege, but a constant duty—"Rejoice in the Lord always. I will say it again: Rejoice" (Philippians 4:4). There is something defective in our religion if it does not fill us with a happiness that is fatal to indifference or despair. If we are acquainted with the redeeming love of Christ, surely there is fire enough in it to keep our hearts warm. The Spirit of God is given to them that ask Him and to be filled with the Spirit is to be borne along by an inspiration which supplies to all our endeavors a strength above our own.

I repeat what was suggested in the extract quoted already from the article on "The Sin of Accidie"—that the secret of spiritual health and happiness is to be engaged in doing good. When religion is confined to the heart and is limited to anxiety about eternal welfare, it is no wonder if it becomes dreary and morbid for like a person who never breathes the fresh air or takes any exercise—we are not fulfilling the conditions of health. But let us interest ourselves in others, let us confess the Savior, let us cultivate Christian fellowship, let us lend a hand to help those who are trying to make the world better and to bring in the kingdom of God and, as the color comes to the cheeks of the one who climbs a mountain, so we will find that doubt and indifference take flight from our souls and that the joy of the Lord is our strength.

PART 2

THE SEVEN CARDINAL VIRTUES

THE SEVEN CARDINAL VIRTUES

"The Seven Deadly Sins" formed the theme of the first part of this book, and it seems natural to follow that course with a section on "The Seven Cardinal Virtues." The idea of the seven deadly sins is that, among the innumerable sins of which human beings may be guilty, there are seven of peculiar virulence from which all the rest can be derived; and, in the same way, the idea of the seven cardinal virtues is that, among the countless excellences with which human character may be adorned, there are seven that overtop the rest, and from which all the rest are derived. The adjective "cardinal" refers especially to this latter point; it signifies that these are the virtues on which all others hinge. For instance, from wisdom six virtues are included according to one ancient author, and no fewer than ten according to another.

The idea of cardinal virtues is an exceedingly old one. It occurs in Plato and Aristotle, descended to the Greek philosophical schools, and from there to the Romans, being prominent in the writings of Cicero and from them it passed to the Fathers of the Church.

The Greeks counted only four cardinal virtues: wisdom, courage, temperance, and justice. According to them, these were the four sides of a perfectly symmetrical character, and whoever possessed them could stand foursquare to all the winds that blow. In the Old Testament Apocrypha, these four are also mentioned, and a

Jewish writer, Philo of Alexandria, of the time of our Lord compares them to the four rivers that watered the garden of Eden—so do these fertilize and adorn human nature. Christianity, however, introduced a nomenclature as well as a conception of virtue of its own. Many virtues are mentioned in the New Testament, but three occur constantly, as comprehending in themselves the whole of Christian character—namely, faith, hope, and charity.

When the church fathers built their systems of dogma, of course they selected the stones out of the quarry of the Bible; but they were also powerfully under the influence of Greek philosophy—especially Aristotle. In constructing an ethical system, they took the triad of virtues from the New Testament and added to it the quartet derived from philosophy, and thus there emerged the seven we discuss in the following pages. Perhaps in thus combining things having diverse origins, they did not sufficiently consider whether the old virtues were not, to some extent, identical with the new; but, for practical purposes, no harm is done if a bit of the ground is gone over twice; and it is of distinct advantage to be reminded that Christian character has a natural foundation, though, of course, even the heathen virtues are modified when they appear in the mosaic of Christian character.

Sometimes the name of cardinal virtues is restricted to the four virtues of the pre-Christian philosophers, whereas the other three are named the Christian or the theological virtues; but certainly the latter are cardinal also—that is, *hinge virtues*—and it is convenient to have a single adjective for designating the whole seven.

⊰WISDOM⊱

Wisdom is the foremost of the virtues. It is the lamp-bearer showing the way to the rest. Its principal business is to identify the goal to which they should all strive, and the point to which the whole course of life should tend.

When Thomas Carlyle was an old man, he said to someone that he was often pondering the first question of the Shorter Catechism, "What is the chief end of man?" with its wonderful answer, "Man's chief end is to glorify God and to enjoy Him forever." Every Scotsman has known this question and answer ever since he can remember, but few may have reflected on the reason why this should be the first question. It is the first because it is taken for granted that the foremost inquiry of a rational being will be about the purpose of its own existence. In point of fact, this is often the last question rather than the first. Still it is a sublime fact that the first seed of thought dropped into the mind of a whole nation should be a question like this, which tends to make those to whom it is addressed ponder on the purpose of life. *Why am I alive? Why should I wish to go on living?* These are the thoughts suggested to the mind by this first question of the catechism, and it is in thoughts like these that wisdom has its birth.

That which in the old language of the catechism is called "the chief end," is exactly the same as that which in modern language we call "the ideal"; and every modern mind can appreciate the importance of the question "What is our ideal?", for no belief has more complete possession of the modern mind than the necessity of ideals, and the maxim is common that, if you wish to find out a person's moral worth, you have to discover his or her ideal.

Perhaps it might be said of many that they have no ideal. And this is their condemnation. They have no object in life; they have never reflected why they are alive; their course is determined, not by their own choice, but by the blind forces of appetite within and of conventionality without. Such may truly be said to be dead while they live; for surely in such a vast and perilous enterprise as the voyage of life the first duty of everyone who claims to be human is to be aware where he or she is going. But, from another point of view, it may be said that every human being has a personal ideal, whether aware of it or not. In every mind, consciously or unconsciously, there forms itself by degrees some supreme desire to which the thoughts are ever tending and toward the attainment of which the endeavors are ever set. It may be pleasure or success, or some special form of one or the other of these. The drunkard is not aware of the hold his vice has on him, but drink is the object to which his reveries and designs are ever bent. The miser does not know himself to be the slave of money, but it absorbs his thoughts by day and his dreams by night. The woman of the world would not confess to herself that social advancement is her idol, but year by year the passion for it burns in her blood and determines her conduct. In this sense, ideals are innumerable, and it is by their crossing and clashing, their vehemence and urgency, that the myriad-colored spectacle of existence is produced. But they are, for the most part, unconscious, or, at least, unavowed.

The ideal of the first answer of the Shorter Catechism is a very high one: "to glorify God and enjoy Him forever." But, if we are to have a conscious and an avowed ideal, how can we pitch it lower? Can we be satisfied without having the approval of God in this life and the prospect of spending our eternity with Him in the life to come? You may alter the name of the ideal. Many in our day would prefer Christ's own name for it—"the kingdom of God"; others might call it Welfare, or Blessedness, or Perfection, but the name signifies little; the essential thing is that we should know and avow what we intend to be and to do in this world, and in which port we intend to arrive when the voyage is finished. This is wisdom.

Wisdom is concerned not only with the goal but the way to it, not only with the end but the means for attaining it, not only with the ideal but with the actual. A pilot guiding a ship upriver in the dark sees afar the shining light that marks his destination; but, if he is to arrive there, he has to mark a hundred lesser lights by which his course from point to point is indicated; and, if he neglects these, his ship will be aground long before he is halfway up the channel. So, suppose you have chosen the goal indicated in the answer to the first question of the Shorter Catechism as your own. This supreme purpose includes many subordinate purposes, such as the development of character; the discharge of your duty as a citizen, as a member of the church, and in the family; your success in business, and so on. In fact, as the pilot has to be watchful at every bend of the course, at every encounter with a passing ship, and at every change in the state of the tide, so must you, as a wise person, choose your path every day and every hour. You must compare and weigh and judge; you must appropriate the good and reject the bad; you must discern what will help and what will hinder; and you must pitch upon the means that will take you, not only to the ultimate end, but to the several halting places by the way.

The Latin name for the virtue which the Greeks called wisdom is prudence, and this change is characteristic. In the process of passing from the one ancient language to the other, ideas frequently lost something of their loftiness and delicacy. The Romans were a practical people, and they aimed low. Taking for granted that the end of life consisted in getting-on, they restricted the task of wisdom to the means of attaining it. Such a debased wisdom has never died out of the world, and Bunyan embodied its characteristics in Mr. Worldly Wiseman. But there is a prudence that is not ignoble, but an essential part of wisdom; if we would reach the end—even the highest end—we must use the means.

We must know the facts of the world. Facts are stubborn things; and we may make them either our friends or our foes, as fire may either be a devouring element or the force that carries us and our burdens through steam-powered travel, and as electricity may either be death-dealing lightning or the power to carry our messages round the globe. We may set nature up against us, or we may convert it into a friend and helper, and wisdom consists in doing the latter. Still more is it displayed in dealing with human nature. We have to realize the purpose of our life, not in a vacuum or a solitude, but in a world of men and women, and every one of those we encounter may either further our aim or retard it. Every human heart is a mystery, and human nature is a great deep. In nothing is wisdom more displayed than in knowing others, and in so treating them that they may favor instead of opposing our advance.

We must know and obey the laws. On all objects and on all events the laws are written in hieroglyphics which the wise can decipher, but the fool misreads or does not see at all. Not only is there a narrow road and a broad road to be chosen once for all, but at every step there is a right and a wrong, and a choice has to be made. Conscience within and God above whisper, "This is the way: walk in it" (Isaiah 30:21); and blessed is the one who walks straight forward, even though at the moment it seems to be into the jaws of hell. But, if reason and conscience and God say, "This way!" and one believes the way to happiness is by walking in the opposite direction, that person is a fool.

✢ ✢ ✢

It was a question discussed of old in the philosophical schools of Greece, whether wisdom can be taught. There is more of an intellectual element in it than in the other virtues, and wisdom has sometimes been so conceived as to make it the peculiar property of those of talent or genius. Nor can it be denied that some natures are from birth more akin to it than others. Who would deny Plato's gift of intuition into the laws of the moral universe or Shakespeare's instinctive discernment of human nature? But, if wisdom consists in the choice of the true end of life and in the use of those means for attaining it placed by Providence at our disposal, then it must be the privilege and the duty of every child of God, and, therefore, it must be capable of being acquired.

How, then, is wisdom to be attained?

Firstly, wisdom is partly attained by precept. There have been many wise people in the world before us, and vast stores of wisdom have been accumulated. These are to be found partly in the tradition that comes down to us by means of speech, as, for instance, in the proverbs which fly from mouth to mouth and descend from parent to child. These "maxims hewn from life" are the concentrated essence of a nation's wisdom, and there is no nation which does not possess proverbs of its own. Our own nation is specially rich in them, and it is one mark of the wise to annex these spontaneously and to speak in proverbs. Then the store of the world's wisdom has been largely garnered in books, and, although a fool may read hundreds of these without becoming wise, anyone with the seed of wisdom will grow wiser by means of books if chosen well. A book like Bacon's *Essays* shows how much wisdom can be packed into a hundred pages; and sometimes a poet, like Burns in his "Letter to a Young Friend," can distill the essence of the wisdom of an entire people into a few lines. In the Apocrypha there is a book entitled the Book of Wisdom, and the name is not undeserved; but it might be more justly applied to such a book as Proverbs or to the Bible as a whole. Several books of the Old Testament are spoken of sometimes as the Wisdom Literature because they frequently deal by name with this subject. They are poetical books, but the prophetical books are in a still higher sense a Wisdom Literature; yet even these pale before the remarks of our Lord and His apostles in the New Testament. Anyone who aims at wisdom should take as a motto the verse in the first chapter of Joshua, applying it to the whole Bible, "Do not let this Book of the Law depart from your mouth; meditate on it day and night, so that you may be careful to do everything written in it. Then you will be prosperous and successful" (Joshua 1:8).

Secondly, *wisdom is learned by practice*. It is, as I have said, partly an intellectual virtue, but it consists much less in knowing than in doing. It is slowly accumulated by experience, and, like the pearl which forms where the bivalve has been wounded, it frequently springs from pain and misfortune. Other virtues shine most attractively in youth, but wisdom is the special ornament of old age; and it compensates for the drawbacks of this period of life.

Best of all, *wisdom is learned through imitation*. "He who walks with the wise grows wise," says Proverbs 13:20, "but a companion of fools suffers harm." It is not, indeed, so easy as such advice might imply to get into the company

of the wise; they have their own friends and companions
and may be jealous of intrusion on their privacy and on
their time; the wise might be making themselves the companions of fools if they kept company with us; and we must
be prepared to pass through the ordeal of a strict inspec-
tion. But there is, at least, One who will not cast us out;
and His friendship is more certain to make us wise than
that of any other. One of the names of the Savior is Wisdom, and He, it is said in Holy Scripture, is made of God
unto us wisdom. He places no bounds to the intimacy we
may seek with Him; and, if we are thus made wise unto
salvation, there is little fear but we shall be welcome to
other wise companionship even in this world, while in the
world to come we may reckon on a humble place in that
society of which it has been written, "Those who are wise
will shine like the brightness of the heavens, and those
who lead many to righteousness, like the stars for ever and
ever" (Daniel 12:3).

⚜COURAGE⚜

There is no name which a well-conditioned mind abhors more than that of coward, and every young man covets a reputation for being courageous. It is a favorite occupation of boyhood, in hours of reverie, to dream of situations in which the dreamer performs heroic exploits and earns the applause of the astonished onlookers. Of course, the probability of anything of the kind ever happening is not seriously entertained even by the boy when he is fully awake, and it disappears altogether as soon as the walls of reality begin to close around the growing mind. But it is good that the dream has been there; the stronger the aspirations after the heroic in a boyish mind the better; in fact, in some shape these ought always to survive; and, although the form of their realization may be totally different from the visions of youth, yet they will receive fulfillment in every true life. Every brave soul retains in its composition to the last a strain of the romantic.

Neither the four virtues of the ancient world nor the three of the Christian world were picked at haphazard out of the total number of human excellences. Although the connection between the two groups may be indeterminate, the connection between the members of each of the groups is closest. Especially is this the case with the subject of the first chapter and that of the present one; and I wish the connection to be noted because the course will make a deeper and more lasting impression if its different members form themselves into an organism in the mind of the reader.

What, then, is the connection between wisdom and courage? Wisdom, as we saw in the last chapter, is chiefly concerned with the object of existence; it fixes on the supreme good which we decide to pursue. Courage is the force by which the obstacles that impede this pursuit are overcome. It is a kind of indignation that blazes out against everything that would prevent it from going where duty calls. It is the club of Hercules, the hammer of Thor, with which we clear the path to the goal.

It is highly important to keep this connection between wisdom and courage in view because it enables us to distinguish between true courage and its counterfeits, of which there are many. No sailor is more resolute in facing the stormy seas than is the pirate in tracking the booty on which he has fixed his greed; but we do not honor the resolution of such a human shark with the name of bravery—we call it ferocity. No confessor, championing the truth in the face of principalities and powers, is more sure of his or her own opinions than is many an ignoramus who, gifted with nothing but self-conceit and a loud voice, shouts down the argument of all opponents; but we do not call such noisy stubbornness by the name of courage—we call it pig-headedness. The assassin of President McKinley took his life in his hands and must have been more certain of having to die for what he was about to do than is the leader of the most desperate forlorn hope on the field of battle, but whatever his master motive may have been—whether it was an immoderate vanity and craving for notoriety, or a malignant hatred of capitalism and a morbid compassion for the poor—we do not count his act a brave one. It sends to the heart no thrill such as a brave act excites but quite the reverse.

The truth is, the raw material of courage is neither beautiful nor admirable. It exists in brutes in greater measure than in humans. No soldier attacks with the violence of the tiger; no hero stands firm with the tenacity of a bulldog. As the clay requires to have another element transfused through it before it can assume shapes of beauty, so the animal instinct requires to have something higher added before it becomes truly admirable. And this addition is that which wisdom supplies, namely, an end worthy of pursuit. Courage is the power of going forward in spite of difficulties to reach a chosen and worthy object.

Although wisdom is the primary virtue in the order of logic, courage is probably the primary one in the order of time. It was the first virtue—the first which humankind exemplified, noticed, and extolled. In both the Greek and Latin languages the very name for virtue itself is manliness, or valor, and the evolutionists would probably demonstrate that all other virtues are derivable from this one.

The original arena of courage was the battlefield. The earliest heroes of all nations were the valiant who performed exploits in defense of their altars and their hearths. The Greek poets and orators never tired of extolling Thermopylae, where three hundred brave warriors rolled back the whole power of the East. The lyre of the Roman poet emitted its most subduing notes when he told of Regulus, who, when sent home to negotiate peace by his captors the Carthaginians, counseled the senate to make no peace but to carry on the war more vigorously and, when his heroic courage had prevailed, went back to Carthage, in fulfillment of his parole, to be exposed to the torrid African sun with his eyelids cut off, and rolled down a steep place in a barrel spiked with nails. "He pushed aside," says the Roman poet, "the embraces of his chaste wife and the kisses of his little children, and would not lift his face from the ground till the trembling senators agreed to his proposal, and then through the ranks of his weeping friends he hastened back to exile, well knowing the tortures which awaited him there, yet as [happy] as if he had been going to one of the retreats of luxury and beauty on the southern shores of his native Italy." In modern times, in like manner, the Scots have their Robert the Bruce, the English their Nelson, the Tyrolese their Andreas Hofer, and the Swiss their Wilhelm Tell. Nor has this primitive sentiment yet died out, as we see by the circle of fame which in our own time has surrounded the names of Moltke and Gordon.

In battle one risks the most precious possession of all—namely, one's own life. All people instinctively cling to life, and dread death as the worst of all evils because it sums up all earthly losses in one; and when they see a General Gordon, with nothing in his hand but the staff of a civilian, going about in his business as coolly as if he were taking the air in a flower garden, they feel for him an admiration which knows no bounds. Here again, however, the question arises, wherein true valor consists. In some cases recklessness may be a mere animal propensity. A celebrated general used to say that in a thousand men there would be fifty ready to run any risk, another fifty ready to run away on any pretext, while the nine hundred were neither brave nor the reverse, and it was a tossup which of the two fifties they would follow. In others it may be the callousness of custom. The veteran enters the breach with much the same indifference with which any other laborer goes about a day's work. Some of the bravest soldiers have been the most timid to begin with, like that one who, when reproached by a rough companion for trembling, replied, "Yes, I am afraid; but, if you had been as afraid as I am, you would have run away long ago." Here we see the true soul of valor peeping out; it is the mettle in a mind inspired by a great end, whether this end be called duty, loyalty, or patriotism. The truly brave is the one who loves some worthy object so much that he or she is willing to risk everything—even life itself—to attain it.

In the eyes of the primitive, the only hero was the warrior. It was a great step in advance when it was recognized that there is a valor of peace no less admirable than that of war. The Roman Cicero said, "The majority consider that military life is superior to that of civilians; but this opinion must be confuted, for in civil affairs there are opportunities of valor even more brilliant than in war." This is the voice of civilization, and the great lesson of modern times.

We know now that the physician, who goes from house to house and bed to bed fighting an epidemic and exposing his own life, and perhaps that of his family, to danger every day, is as worthy of admiration as the soldier who walks with intrepidity up to the cannon's mouth. It is not without justification that the fireman, rescuing women and children from burning houses at the risk of being crushed by falling beams or tumbling walls, is as popular in the reading of the young as the soldier or the sailor. The politician who maintains the cause of humanity in the face of the frowns of the multitude and in spite of the danger of being turned out of office; the journalist who refuses, notwithstanding a diminishing circulation, to make her newspaper the organ of a public opinion she believes to be wrong; the judge who sentences a titled favorite of society to the hulks with the same impartiality with which he would dispose of an ordinary criminal — such are the heroes of civil life. But we must bring heroism down to still more lowly acts, for the pure ore of courage is often most abundant where it is least discerned by untrained eyes. The widow who, when her husband has been taken from her side, does not surrender herself to despair but resolves to face the world alone and bring up her children in honesty; the man who has failed in business, but, instead of forever harking back to the glory of his prosperous days, adjusts his outlay to his new circumstances and refuses to let go of self-respect; the policeman who rushes into a barricaded room to grapple with a madman — these are the brave of the modern type.

The bravery of soldiers is a momentary effort. By one charge, which is over and done in an hour, they earn the admiration and the gratitude of their fellow citizens. But the most difficult heroism is that which is long-continued, the strain never relaxing year after year, and the struggle requiring to be constantly renewed. The pressure of conventionality is constant. It is continually seeking to wear down our individuality and reduce us to the level of mere specimens of a common type. Even at school the force of practice and opinion is tyrannical, and the student dreads being different from his or her peers. As life goes on, the tendency to be a mere echo of others becomes more and more pronounced, and any deviation from what society prescribes and expects is treated as a crime. It is said that in city life especially this obliteration of individuality is the rule; while those in the country grow up with their own features and can express their own opinions, in the town we are all turned off on the same pattern, as if we had dropped from a machine. Oh, the weary repetition of the streets, the monotony of the crowds that stream together from the gates of our public works, the artificial and mechanical sameness of the drawing room! It is a lifelong struggle for a human being now to be able to say, "I am what I am," to look the world in the face and, without oddity or bounce, maintain and express an individual mind.

For this a person must be often alone—able to enjoy solitude. Many are afraid of themselves and betake themselves instinctively to crowds; but it is in the crowd that the features of individuality are rubbed off, and one becomes a cipher and a nonentity. It may seem a strange test of courage to set up, but it is a genuine one, when we say that those are bravest who can look into their inmost selves steadily and long in the face without blenching.

No arena affords greater scope for courage than religion. So it has been from the beginning. If you wish to see a hero, look at David approaching Goliath, not in the armor of Saul but in the faith of the God of Jacob; or look at Elijah, on Carmel, standing alone against the world. In the New Testament look at Stephen on the field of martyrdom, or at St. Paul passing through a hundred deaths. Every century since then has had its martyrs down to those, numbering thousands, who have recently sealed their testimony with their blood in China. There is no extreme of courage beyond martyrdom; yet often have tender and delicate women for the sake of their faith, and for the sake of their Lord, braved the worst that the hellish ingenuity of inquisitors or the brutality of the roughest soldiery could invent. This is the most perfect illustration of sacrifice for a noble end.

The necessity for courage is inherent in the Christian religion, for the world is instinctively its enemy. There are innumerable degrees and forms of opposition—sometimes it is violent and brutal, ready to grasp at fire and sword in order to annihilate what it abhors; at other times it is scornful, using the weapons of satire and comedy; and there are times when it actually professes Christianity itself, and affects only to object to a spirituality which is fantastic and an austerity which is extreme; but everywhere and always the spirit of the world is hostile to the spirit of Christ, and the courage requisite to stand up against it may sometimes be greater when the opposition is soft-spoken than when it is boisterous.

Another thing that makes courage a necessity to the Christian is that our Lord and Master demands testimony from us. "You are my witnesses" (Isaiah 43:12), says Jesus to one and all who have believed on Him for salvation; and the word "witnesses" is the same as "martyrs." Every Christian is a possible martyr. Circumstances are conceivable in which we would either have to lose our life or cast away our hope; and the world is not yet so improved that anyone who is loyal to the Lord should be able to escape scot-free. There is a great deal more persecution still going on in the world than many people are aware. In every city there are works and shops where anyone making a decided profession of Christianity has to run the gauntlet of ridicule and annoyance; and there are homes, too, in which, under the safe cover of what ought to be tender relationships, stabs of aversion and malignity are dealt in the dark.

This is the cross of Christ, and it takes courage to bear it. But let none who are bearing it be ashamed, for it makes them the associates of the heroes of every age. The greatest of all martyrs was Jesus Himself. Never was there purer courage than His; and it was courage even unto death. He bore the cross and despised the shame, and there is no way of getting so near Him as suffering for His sake. Coleridge tells a striking story of a young officer who confided to him that in his first battle he was absolutely demoralized with fear, till his general, Sir Alexander Ball, the friend of Coleridge, grasped his fingers and said, "I was just the same the first time I was in a battle," when, at that touch and these words, his timidity vanished in a moment and never returned. It is an instructive as well as an affecting incident, suggesting what the mature might do for beginners in the warfare of the Lord. But the best encouragement is in the touch and the word of the Lord Himself. He can say, "I trembled once like you," as He remembers Gethsemane and the wilderness of temptation. "For we do not have a high priest who is unable to sympathize with our weaknesses, but we have one who has been tempted in every way, just as we are—yet was without sin. Let us then approach the throne of grace with confidence, so that we may receive mercy and find grace to help us in our time of need" (Hebrews 4:15-16).

⚜TEMPERANCE⚜

Let us begin, as in the last chapter, with a word or two about the connection.

Wisdom, courage, temperance—these are the first three of the seven cardinal virtues, and they are closely connected with one another. Wisdom chooses the end of life—the goal that has to be reached. Courage fights down the enemies and overcomes the obstacles that present themselves in the path to the goal. Temperance has to do with the enemies within—with the lusts and passions that war against the soul.

Many must feel that for them the latter are the real enemies. No doubt in everyone's lot there is a share of temptations coming from without; but a whole army storming on the citadel from the outside is less formidable than a single enemy within the walls. And who has not such an enemy? The danger of temptation lies not so much in its own strength as in an affinity for it within the soul of the tempted, for this is a traitor that conveys the key of the gates to the attacking forces. Who among us is not aware of some weakness within that gives temptation its chance and its advantage? In some of us this native or acquired bent toward certain sins may be so strong that we hardly need to be tempted, but may almost be said to tempt the tempter. Which of us would like to unveil to the public eye all that goes on in our own imagination in hours of solitude and reverie? Are we not ashamed of it?

Do we not wonder at ourselves? Like serpents weltering in the dark depths of some obscene pit, lust and passion turn and twist, inflate themselves and rage with mad violence; and they lift up their heads after being wounded apparently unto death a hundred times. It is with the control of these unruly elements in human nature that temperance has to do; for, if they are not overcome, the goal of wisdom will certainly be missed.

There are many voices at present that deny temperance is a virtue. Holding the only law of life to be development, they demand for every power the fullest expansion, and they ask why capacities of enjoyment have been bestowed on us by nature if they are not to be satisfied. Often has the thirst for strong drink been thus vindicated; and bacchanalian poets have poured glittering shafts of contempt on those who avoid too scrupulously the boundaries of intoxication or try to impose abstinence on others. With nearly equal frequency has the privilege of nature been claimed against the Christian law of chastity, which has been represented as an outrage on reason and a cruel and arbitrary limitation of the joys of existence.

But such doctrines are contradicted by their fruits. The unbridled indulgence of desire soon ends in both physical and moral exhaustion. For a short time, indeed, the remonstrances of reason may be drowned by the revelry of liberty; the songs of carousing pleasure may shake the air with applause; goblets may foam, eyes sparkle, and laughter echo; but soon the roses wither, and in place of the beaming eye there grins the horrible eye socket. No one has ever given more eloquent and daring expression to the claims of liberty in the use of the wine cup than the poet Robert Burns; but his own end, in its inexpressible sadness, was a commentary of nature which even the most thoughtless could not mistake. If among the masters of song there is one in modern times who, for the perfection and inevitability of the lyric note, deserves to be placed in the same rank as Burns, it is the German poet, Heine. He employed his transcendent gifts in glorifying and vindicating the rehabilitation of the flesh; but the long years he spent at the close of life, buried alive in his mattress grave, as he called it, taught all Europe, with a force and a pathos which nothing could have exceeded, that the end of those things is death.

On the contrary, experience shows how beautiful and beneficial, when subject to control and restrained to their own time, place, and function, are even those parts of human nature that, when uncontrolled, tend most inevitably to corruption and destruction. When fire breaks loose and rages on its own account, it carries swift destruction in its course; but, when restricted within certain bounds, it warms our rooms and cooks our food, illuminates our towns and drives our locomotives. In the same way, water, when in flood, roots up trees, carries away houses, and sweeps the crops from the fields; but, when confined within its banks, drives the wheel and floats the barge and rejoices the eye, either by its placid flow or by the splendors of the cataract. So the very qualities that, when unregulated, waste and brutalize life may, when subjected to the control of temperance, be its fairest ornaments. Thus the person who is prone to conversation may, by making unrestrained use of that power, gradually become a bore, from whose chattering everyone flees; whereas the restrained use of the tongue would cause that person to be looked upon as the possessor of a delightful gift, by which all who knew him or her would profit. Temper, when indulged without restraint, is a kind of madness, which transmutes the one who is overmastered by it into a demon, but when checked and disciplined, it turns into the sensitiveness of a person of honor. Nothing is, in this respect, more remarkable than the instinct of sex — one of the parts of our nature with which the virtue of temperance has most to do; when emancipated from the law of God and the law of modesty, it brutalizes more quickly and more completely than any other form of indulgence; but, when, obedient to the laws of nature and of God, it blossoms into virgin and then wedded love, it is the very essence of those charities and joys that make the home the center of attraction to the heart as well as the basis of the whole fabric of society.

Thus is intemperance demonstrated to be vicious and temperance to be virtuous by their patent and undeniable effects.

Sometimes the doctrines just referred to that demand emancipation from all restraint are called *Greek*, whereas those which insist upon control are called *Hebraic*. Heine, in his prose writings, which are hardly less brilliant than his poetry, often speaks of the whole of modern history as being a conflict between these two tendencies; and, in the same sense, a distinguished Scottish minister published a book under the title of *Culture and Restraint*. Culture is the Greek ideal—the free and full development of every part of human nature; and restraint is the Hebrew ideal—the control by law and will of the too volatile and violent desires.

For these names there is a certain amount of justification. The Greeks looked at one side of the shield and the Hebrews at the other; doubtless the tendency of each to do so was due to natural temperament. Both tendencies were carried to excess: the Greek civilization allowed an excess of indulgence and fell accordingly into shameful decay; the Hebraic element in Christianity has frequently put a ban on legitimate pleasure and taught that mere abstinence, for its own sake, is meritorious in the sight of God. Aestheticism is the extreme in the one direction, asceticism in the other.

Those wise among the Greeks, however, were well aware that restraint was necessary; and, while their watchword was development, they knew that the harmony of all the parts could not be secured without the rigid suppression of violent passions. Beauty was the Greek ideal, but beauty means everything in its own place and every member fulfilling its own function. In like manner, the Hebrews, while insisting upon restraint, did so only with a view to culture. The base and inferior must be restrained if a chance is to be given to what is more excellent. If ever there was a Hebrew, it was St. Paul, but in his

wonderful parable of the body and the members, in
1 Corinthians 12, he shows himself to be both in love
with moral beauty and well aware of the essential principles of aesthetics.

The necessity for temperance is based on the fact that
the constitution of humans is composed of many parts of
different degrees of value and dignity, on the harmonious
working together of which happiness depends. It is as in
an army, where there are many degrees, from the general
to the private soldier. How would it do in a battle if every
soldier were to act on his own initiative, no one waiting for
the word of command? Even if every man were loyal and
brave, and acting for the best as he understood it, the whole
army would become a scene of immeasurable disorder and
fall an easy prey to the enemy. It is as in a ship or a boat
where every sailor or rower has his own place and his own
work. In a boat on the Cam or the Isis, when the prize for
oarsmanship is about to be decided, how would it do if
every oarsman considered it his right to let himself go and
pull with all the strength at his command? This would cor-
respond exactly with the theory of those who hold that
every part of human nature is entitled to unrestrained
development; but it would work havoc on the river and
entail inevitable defeat. If there is to be any hope of victory,
every oarsman has to consider his neighbors and keep his
eye on the coxswain; he must do nothing for his own glory
or gratification but regulate the amount of force he puts
into every stroke by a calculation of what is demanded of
him at that particular point at that particular moment.

So in ourselves there is the broad distinction of the

body with its parts and the soul with its powers. The body has its own dignity and its own rights, but the soul is manifestly superior. Yet the body is constantly endeavoring to assert itself and get the upper hand. Hence the need to keep the body under control. Then, among the powers of the soul there is the utmost variety, with many gradations of dignity. Some powers are near akin to the body. Such are the appetites, of which the chief are these three—the appetite for eating, the appetite for drinking, and the appetite for sex. These are common to humans as well as animals and are specially apt to become unruly and violent. So much is this the case that the word *temperance* is sometimes restricted to the control of these alone. At the opposite extreme from these animal propensities are such imperial powers as conscience and reason, while in between come other feelings, some of which are more and some less noble. Thus, the feeling of reverence we entertain for God and the feelings of affection of which the chief arena is the home are noble, while there are many feelings, such as the desire for money or the desire for praise, which, though not base in themselves, tend to baseness.

Temperance, then, is the control of the lower by the higher powers; or it is the force of will by which all are kept in their own places and compelled to do their own work. When the habit of temperance is thoroughly formed, every excess is instantly checked and every reluctant power promptly stimulated. Thus the whole being develops steadily and acts harmoniously; and the effects of temperance ought to be internal peace and external beauty.

✤ ✤ ✤

The self-control just described can be neither won nor maintained without severe and continuous effort, accompanied by many a failure and many a new beginning. In more than one passage of his writings, St. Paul speaks of his own heart as a scene of civil war, the more earthly principles contending with the more spiritual, like a rebel army with the forces of the crown; and of this struggle no one who breathes is wholly ignorant. Each of us has our own besetting sin. It may be a tendency bequeathed by ancestors, such as a cursed craving for drink; it may be a peculiarity of temperament, such as a liability to uncontrolled fits of temper; it may be a habit acquired in years of youthful folly, which still clings although the past has been blotted out by repentance; it may even be allied to what is noble and good, like some forms of pride. But there it is, and we have to wrestle with it for our salvation. It seems to me there is encouragement in the reflection that this conflict is going on, in one form or other, in every heart; this should make us sympathetic toward others and hopeful about ourselves. Others whose distress has been as desperate as ours have conquered; why shouldn't we? We are compassed about with a great cloud of witnesses.

Every time the unruly appetite is indulged, it becomes stronger, and its next victory will be more easily won; but every time the will, directed by reason and conscience, gets the upper hand, it is itself strengthened, and its next effort will be more prompt and successful. Such is the law of the battle; and it is by the growth of the will in vigor, swiftness, and perseverance that victory is secured.

Yes, this secures the victory, but not this alone. St. Paul, in one of his epistles, compares this moral struggle to the games so renowned in ancient Greece; and he says that everyone taking part in these games was temperate in all things. The training undergone by athletes in preparation is proverbial. In Greece the fixed period for this purpose was ten months; and the discipline was most severe. It could not be relaxed for a single day; otherwise the benefit of the preceding time was lost, and some rival would get to the front. But the candidates for the honors of the arena did not go about from day to day, all the ten months, complaining of their hard lot. They took it as a matter of course; and what they thought and talked about was the prize they expected to win—the chaplet of green leaves to be placed on their brows amidst the applause of admiring Greece; the wall of their native town to be thrown down at the place where they were conducted back by their rejoicing fellow citizens; the privileges of many kinds which they would enjoy for the remainder of their days. Temperance becomes easy and even exhilarating when the prize to be won by it is great enough. "They do it to get a crown that will not last; but we do it to get a crown that will last forever" (1 Corinthians 9:25). What father of a family has not observed with reverence and amazement the superiority to the most urgent demands of the body, such as sleep, exhibited by a mother when nursing an ailing child? Temperance is easy when there is a strong enough affection involved.

The terms of the moral struggle we wage may be suddenly and completely altered by the entrance into our consciousness of the prize to be won or of the person for whose sake the sacrifices have to be endured. And if the prize and the person have the same name—Christ!—the victory is difficult, and yet it is easy. To obtain control over an unruly passion or a besetting sin may be painful as the plucking out of a right eye and the cutting off of a right hand. Jesus does not deny it; the words are His own. Yet His yoke is easy and His burden light. How is the contradiction between these two statements to be reconciled? The answer to that question is the secret of the gospel, and blessed are they to whom it has been revealed.

⚜JUSTICE⚜

In the preceding chapters I have taken pains to point out the connection between one virtue and another; the three already discussed—wisdom, courage and temperance—are very closely related. But the connection of the fourth, justice, with the other three is not so close. Those are virtues of personal character; this has respect chiefly to other people. No doubt, without wisdom, courage, and temperance, one cannot cultivate justice with any success. On the other hand, the earnest pursuit of justice will react favorably on these other virtues, but, on the whole, while the three first cause the one who is cultivating them to look continually within, this fourth involves looking continually without, and to consider what is owed to other people.

For *justice* is the giving everyone their due. It is the virtue of humans, not as we stand by ourselves, but in our place in society; and, in order to understand our whole duty in regard to it, we must remember our relations to all other human beings—superiors, inferiors, and equals—and our connection with each circle of the social organization, such as the family, the city, the nation, and the church. As we relate to creatures beneath and above ourselves, besides those who are our equals, the idea of justice might be stretched to include behavior to the lower animals and duties toward God. Indeed, in some modern books, cruelty to animals is discussed under justice, while in the ethical systems of the scholars, and especially in the

Summa of Thomas Aquinas—the book recommended before all others to the study of Christendom by the present Pope—the latter forms the greater part of justice, the worship of God in all its branches being discussed in connection with it; but, on the whole, it is better to limit the scope of justice to the relations of human beings to each other.

This is, in itself, a wide field, for it comprehends the mutual duties of parents and children, husbands and wives, brothers and sisters, friends, neighbors, clergy and laity, employers and employed, rulers and subjects, and others too numerous to be mentioned. If anyone were a model in all these respects, that person would be perfect. Hence justice has often been spoken of as the whole of virtue, and Aristotle, in an unwonted access of enthusiasm, speaks of it as being more beautiful than the morning or the evening star.

While the definition of justice as the rendering to everyone their due seems a very simple one, it is in reality not so simple as it looks. This you realize as soon as you begin to ask what is due anyone in particular. Every such question is complicated by the question hidden in it, "What is *my* due?"—for the bias in favor of self too often confuses the verdict. You may lay down a proposition like that embodied in the American Declaration of Independence, that everyone has an inalienable right to life, liberty, and the pursuit of happiness, but you are immediately pulled up by questions like these: "Is that man entitled to life who has taken the life of another?" or "Is a lunatic to be allowed liberty?" or "Does not many a person's pursuit of happiness involve misery for others?" In short, what is anyone's due, and especially, what is one's own due in any relationship of life, can frequently be ascertained only by close and dispassionate inquiry. In order to be trained not only to perform acts of justice but to have a habit of justice, ready to act on every occasion, we are required to put ourselves to more than one school of justice and learn the lessons there imparted. Let us inquire what these schools are.

THE JUSTICE OF THE LAW

So essential is justice for the welfare of all that, wherever people have risen, even in a slight degree, above the savage state, they have employed their best wisdom to declare what justice is and united their strength to enforce it. In early Rome the Twelve Tables were set up in the marketplace, where they could be read by everyone; they told in the plainest words the duties of a citizen and the penalties for breaking them. As civilization advanced, nations formed parliaments for the purpose of defining the rights of the different classes in the community; lawcourts were erected, judges and juries established, and lawyers trained to apply to particular cases the law of the land; while the whole apparatus of prisons and punishments grew to sharpen in the public mind the consciousness of the majesty of the law.

In every country these institutions form a school to which the citizens are put, and in which they learn almost unconsciously multitudes of things which they must do and multitudes of things which they must not do. In most cases, the schooling takes effect almost as perfectly as the schooling of nature by which everyone learns very early in life not to stand in the way of a falling body or to bring the hand too near a fire. Most of us have never been in the clutches of the law of the land, and it may not occur to us once in a year that this is a danger we have to avoid. But for all that, the law has been our schoolmaster, teaching us to do no wrong to our neighbor and to fulfill the promises we have made. Our unawareness of the law only proves how well its work has been done.

THE JUSTICE OF PUBLIC OPINION

The law of the land in any modern state is an embodiment of the experience of centuries, during which multitudes of the acutest minds have been giving their best strength to define what justice is. In the law of our own land, streams of wisdom mingle, derived both from the classical nations and from our Teutonic (or Germanic) ancestors. Yet, with all that has been done, the law of the land is an extremely imperfect embodiment of justice, and one might remain securely outside the clutches of the law and yet be the exact reverse of a just person.

Of the holes in the network of the law of the land, a striking illustration was supplied a short time ago in one of our cities. A man who had occupied a high office in the municipality was summoned into court to answer for a use of his position which, if it became common, would corrupt the administration of the city through and through; but it turned out that what he was charged with doing is no offense against any law in the statute book. Of course I am expressing no opinion as to whether the particular person accused was guilty or not of what was alleged against him, but the case is a curious instance of the imperfection of the law of the land.

Nor is it always the greatest wrongs which the public machinery of justice is directed against, while those it neglects are trivial in comparison. On the contrary, the law often strains at a gnat while it swallows a camel. For example, if anyone were to defraud his neighbor of a penny, the law would lay hold of him and set its whole machinery of police, judges, lawyers, and prisons in motion for his punishment; but the same person might, by the arts of temptation carried on for years, make his neighbor's son a drunkard, or his daughter still worse, and yet escape altogether the notice of the law. That is to say, you may not touch your neighbor's purse, but you may break his heart with impunity as far as the law of the land is concerned.

This shows the need of a stricter school of justice, and this is furnished by public opinion. A person may stay out of the hands of the police, and the law may never have a word to say against him, but society may know him to be guilty of acts which it sternly disapproves and will not suffer to be perpetrated with impunity. He is not fined or imprisoned, but society frowns on him, he loses his character, and the doors through which access is obtained to the pleasures and honors of life are shut in his face. Thus silently, but sternly, does public opinion punish persons known to covet another man's wife and those who commit adultery. On the whole, this is a salutary check on passion and selfishness, while it does much to render society a more habitable place than it would otherwise be.

THE SCHOOL OF CONSCIENCE

Public opinion, like the law of the land, leaves holes in the network of justice which it weaves. In fact, much worse can be said of it: It not infrequently commands what it ought to forbid and forbids what it ought to command. In illustration of this may be adduced the law of honor which, not long ago, forbade any member of the upper class to decline a challenge to engage in a duel; at the opposite extreme of society, it is still considered dishonorable not to treat visitors to strong drink on New Year's day. Of course, it might be alleged against the law of the land, too, that it has often commanded what it was wrong to do and forbidden what was right, as, for instance, when the early Christians were forbidden to worship the Savior and commanded, on pain of death, to bend the knee to the images of heathen divinities; however, a false verdict of public opinion is more difficult to combat than a wrong statute.

The appeal from it, however, is to the conscience of the individual, in which there is erected another school of justice, and a very venerable one. Let us, when not sure what is right or wrong, retire with the question into the solitude of our own hearts, let us rid ourselves of passion and party spirit, and let us ask what we ought to do; provided we really wish to learn the truth, we will seldom fail to ascertain what is our duty. It is a far finer and more severe type of morality that is taught in this school than in that either of public opinion or the law of the land; and it is the great object of religion to strengthen the conscience, teaching people to feel that, confronted by it alone, they are in a more august presence than in any law court, however high, or in a whole theater of spectators. It was to the conscience Jesus appealed when He framed the Golden Rule, "So in everything, do to others what you would have them do to you" (Matthew 7:12). This is the soul of justice.

THE JUSTICE OF CHRIST

As I have just quoted the Golden Rule, it might be thought we had already obtained Christ's contribution to justice. Jesus was a moralist, contending earnestly for righteousness and fair play between people and classes; He was the heir and the successor of the prophets—those stern denouncers of wrong—and He gave us many rules of justice, this golden one among them; yet this was not His only contribution to this cause.

There are some things that make it easy to render to certain persons all that is their due, or even more. In railway traveling everyone has noticed the attention paid by guards and porters to those traveling first-class. When royalty is in any city, all the arrangements of traffic give way to its convenience, and the citizens vie with one another in placing their services at the disposal of the royal visitors. There is not a town in the world where the well dressed do not receive more courtesy than the ragged.

This is the way of human nature. In many cases it may be contemptible, but it is at least fair to take advantage of it on behalf of those at the opposite extreme of the social scale. Jesus did so. He endeavored to secure fair treatment for the common people by raising the universal estimate of them. If the poor are treated without consideration because they are invested with no distinction and dignity to arrest the eye, the treatment they receive will be improved by anything which secures for them respect and reverence. Now, to the mind that has taken in the teachings of Christ, the very humblest belong to that humanity which He took into His heart and for which He gave His life; and it is impossible thus to see others through Christ's eyes—to see God in them, in short—without having a fine and powerful motive for treating them with justice.

As the discussion of our theme has been rather abstract in this chapter, it may be advisable to finish with a practical illustration, and this I will take from the great struggle between capital and labor which is surging on every hand at the present time. What would the four teachers say about what is due by employer to employed, and what is due by employed to employer?

Firstly, the teaching of the law of the land is very brief but decisive. It simply says to the master, "Pay what you owe," and to the servant, "You should not steal." And, simple as this teaching is, there are those to whom it is the thunder of God.

Secondly, public opinion goes a good deal beyond this, though its voice is divided. There is a public opinion of employers, which the employer hears perhaps too exclusively, and there is a public opinion of the employed, which the employee hears perhaps too exclusively. The former urges the stern application of the law of supply and demand, while the latter counsels to take advantage of the employers' necessities. There is a wider public opinion that decides more impartially: It frowns upon the employer who does not at least try to provide the best conditions of labor, and it censures the mechanic or laborer who does only enough to get by, instead of the best. The wider public opinion is imperfectly informed, and therefore makes mistakes; but, on the whole, the influence that it wields is invigorating.

Employers and employees can also appeal to the third tribunal mentioned—their own consciences. Let them ask there what God wishes them to do, and what they would wish others would do to them if their places were exchanged; and then, if they are loyal to the decisions of their consciences, they can hold up their heads and brave public opinion, however hostile and unanimous.

Last of all, what is the message of Christian principle to masters and servants? It will remind the former that servants have an immortal destiny, and it will constrain them to minimize or abolish things, like Sabbath labor and excessive hours, which secularize and brutalize; while servants, as they toil, will hear a voice behind them saying, "Whatever you do, work at it with all your heart, as working for the Lord, not for men" (Colossians 3:23).

I do not mean to say that even with all these sources of light the question of justice will always be an easy one. The reciprocal rights of corporate bodies are particularly difficult to define. But, at all events, it is by letting the instructions of these different teachers play upon the mind that the level of public justice will be raised and the individual prepared for appearing before that solemn tribunal, where the sentences of this world will all be revised and a verdict pronounced from which there will be no appeal.

⚜ FAITH ⚜

In the opening chapter I explained how the cardinal virtues came to be reckoned as seven. The idea of cardinal virtues belongs to the ancient world, as it existed before the appearance of Christianity; but the classical thinkers counted only four—wisdom, courage, temperance, and justice—the four already discussed. But Christianity, when it appeared, gave the foremost places among the virtues, not to these four which were the choice of the philosophers, but to the three known to every reader of the New Testament—faith, hope, and love. It was much later, after Christians also had begun to be philosophers, that the ancient quartet and the Christian trio were joined, so as to produce the seven virtues as we now think of them.

Few things indicate more clearly how great was the change effected by Christianity on the thinking of the world than the fact that it adopted an entirely new set of virtues; for virtues are simply excellences of humankind. The change indicates that the type of character that Christianity tries to produce is radically different from that aimed at by pagan philosophy, and someone has truly said that the final test of every human system or institution is the kind of person it produces.

It might be argued, indeed, that Christianity did not change the virtues but only altered their names. Thus, it might be maintained, with some show of reason, that faith is simply wisdom under another name, that hope is to a large extent identical with courage, and that love has a considerable resemblance to justice. But, while in each of these cases there is a certain likeness, the unlikeness is more obvious, and we must, I think, conclude that Christianity taught humankind to admire a different set of excellences from those set up for the admiration of the ancient world, and that the character it strives to form is a different kind. I may be reminded, indeed, that Christianity has adopted the pagan virtues as its own. But it has adopted them *in addition* to its own; and the three new ones are its own choice in a sense in which the four old ones are not.

It is not, indeed, to be thought that Christianity created these three virtues; it is not to be thought that human beings did not exercise faith, hope, and love before Christianity appeared. People have always believed and hoped and loved. But what Christianity did was to recognize the value and importance of these mental acts or habits; it supplied them with new objects on which to exercise their powers. Faith, hope, and love are the taproots of the plant we call people, but Christianity transplanted the tree into new soil.

Of the three distinctly Christian or theological virtues, as they are sometimes called, the first is faith.

✜ ✜ ✜

The eleventh chapter of Hebrews begins with the most express definition of *faith* given in Scripture—it being defined as "being sure of what we hope for and certain of what we do not see" (Hebrews 11:1)—a brilliant attempt is made to represent the whole history of religion as a process of which faith was the inspiring principle. The heroes of the Old Testament are made to march past in long procession, their exploits are enumerated, and in every case these are attributed to faith, as if this had been the power which produced religion and all its manifestations. In the New Testament faith occupies a foremost place, especially in the writings of St. Paul. The apostles were all aware that in Christ a great new force had entered the world, and faith was the element by which it was appropriated. When in modern times, after centuries of observation, Christianity was rediscovered at the Reformation and preached afresh to the nations by Luther, Calvin, Knox, and the other reformers, faith again became the watchword, and it was through the reappearance of this virtue in people's hearts and in their characters that the rejuvenation of Europe took place.

After that great movement subsided, a stage of development ensued in which faith became an object of speculation more than a living power. People inquired about its nature and disputed with one another about the elements of which it is composed. Thus many strange opinions came to prevail, some of which hang, like cobwebs, about the general mind to this day. Thus in the eighteenth century, when religion was at the lowest ebb in England and Scotland, faith was understood to be the habit of taking on credit dogmas which the mind could not understand, and this submission to the authority of the Bible or the church was supposed to be exceedingly meritorious. But anything more unlike faith, as it is represented in the Bible or as it has prevailed in the heroic periods of religion, it would be difficult to conceive. If in the minds of any there still lingered any remains of the notion that faith is a shutting of the eyes of reason and a blind trusting to authority, I advise you to sweep such rubbish out of your minds. Religion wants to shut no one's eyes; its mission is to *open* them.

It was in opposition to that view of faith that the evangelical doctrine was developed in which most of us were brought up. In evangelical preaching faith held a very prominent and honorable place. Those who can remember the more earnest type of preaching prevalent a generation ago will easily recall the frequency of the appeal, "Only believe, and you shall be saved." But there was a tendency to narrow faith to a single point and to restrict it to a single act, namely, trust in the sacrifice of Christ for the forgiveness of sin. But, however important this may be, it is far from expressing the whole genius of faith. If you go back to a character like Luther and listen to him speaking about faith, as he was incessantly doing, you realize that in him it was the bursting forth of a spring of energy, which spread sunshine and fruitfulness over the entire landscape; it was a habit of the whole person, the actions of which kept all the functions healthy and happy. Faith is wronged when it is conceived as something demanded of us on pain of perdition; it is the most natural, the most health-giving and joy-giving of all experiences.

If I might attempt a definition of faith, I should be inclined to call it *the response of people to God* to His revelations, His promises, and His offers.

✛ ✛ ✛

As has been already said, faith did not come into the world with Christianity, and it is not even peculiar to religion. Faith is a human function, which every human being is exercising every day in regard to multitudes of objects. Whatever lies beyond the range of our own immediate observation is an object of faith. How do those of us who have never been out of Europe know that such places as Africa, Asia, and America exist? It is by believing the testimony of those who have been there; it is by seeing objects not produced in this country and inferring that there must be other continents besides Europe from which they come. Our knowledge of all the events which have happened in this world before our own generation is due to faith—we believe the testimony of those who have placed them on record. And all our knowledge of what is taking place in the world today, except that which is recognized by our own five senses, is obtained in the same way—by testimony, which we accept by faith.

Thus you see how vast is the sweep of faith, and how large a part it plays in everyday life. Of course, testimony has to be sifted. It is not all worthy of belief; some of it is true and some false; and it is the part of the wise to sever the wheat from the chaff, believing only that which is deserving of credence.

Now, among the various testimonies which come to us from many quarters, inviting us to believe in the existence of things we have never seen, there is the testimony of God, certifying to us His own existence and His character. His testimony takes many forms. Partly it is in His works—"For since the creation of the world God's invisible qualities . . . have been clearly seen, being understood from what has been made" (Romans 1:20); partly it is in His providence, for we know that we have not brought ourselves into existence, and that the sweetness of life which we taste is not of our own procuring; partly it is in conscience, where a holy and righteous will, above our own, is daily announcing itself. We are quite entitled to test these evidences; this is our prerogative as reasonable beings. But, if they stand the test, then this Supreme Being is entitled to the homage of our soul—to our admiration, trust, and worship—and this is faith.

Have you ever thought what a change it would make if you believed with all your heart and soul and strength and mind that God is? This one belief would alter everything. Some may even think that it would change too much: If we realized God as He really is, we could think of nothing else. This I do not admit. The thought of God should be to the best of our thinking like the sky to other objects of the landscape—always there, blue, serene, unifying. In His presence, constantly and steadily realized, everything would find its right place; it would be easy to do right and difficult to do wrong. In fact, the problem of life would be solved. Alas, we lose sight of Him; earthly objects shut Him out; we often do not even wish to retain Him in our knowledge because of the imperativeness of His claims on our conscience. But it is the office of faith to overcome this godlessness, saying, in the words of the psalm, "I have set the Lord always before me" (Psalm 16:8).

✤ ✤ ✤

God does not merely stand at a distance, silently appeal-
ing to people through His works: He comes near and
speaks in intelligible words; and His words are promises.

It will be remembered how large a part was played by
the divine promises in the experience of Abraham, the
father of the faithful. God promised him a land and a seed
and a blessing; and the faith of Abraham was exhibited
in laying hold of these promises. In order to do so, he had
to let the world go—for the abandonment of things prized
by the natural heart is always involved in the grasping of
those things to which faith applies itself—but he steadily
followed the star of the promise wherever it led him.
Among the successors of Abraham, this cleaving to a
divine promise through good and bad report, through fair
weather and foul, was so prominent a characteristic of
faith that the writer of the eleventh chapter of Hebrews
sums up their biographies in the words, "All these people
were still living by faith when they died. They did not
receive the things promised; they only saw them and welcomed them from a distance. And they admitted that they
were aliens and strangers on earth" (Hebrews 11:13). And
at all times the life of faith is one of response to the
promises. These are contained in the Word of God. The
reading of God's Word is one of the most native habits of
a Christian life; and the traffic which the soul thereby
keeps up with God consists to a large extent in appropri-
ating the promises.

But the great promise to which faith attaches itself is

that of the life to come. Of immortality humans have dim intimations apart from special revelation; and some thinkers, like Socrates and Plato, before the advent of Christ and apart from the Bible, followed such natural light as was vouchsafed to them with a wistful and noble eagerness. But it is in the Word of God that the unveiling of life to come has taken place, and in Jesus Himself, who has spoken to us distinctly of the mansions intended for our future habitation as one who has been there and is familiar with them. It is, therefore, to His blessed words, above all others, that faith responds when it rises up to claim possession of its heritage.

This action of faith, also, has to overcome obstacles. Not only may doubt arise as to whether even the testimony of Christ is credible, but the things that are temporal engross our time and attention, and, above all, we shrink in cowardice from the kind of life imperatively demanded of us if we really have immortal destiny. Who does not feel that it would change everything to believe wholeheartedly in immortality? It would supply a totally new standard of values: Many things which the world prizes and pursues would become despicable, and many things which the world neglects would become objects of ardent pursuit. The world to come, because invisible, is to the multitude as good as nonexistent, but it may shine as attractively before the eyes of the soul for a lifetime as the prize does for the moment in the eyes of the competitor in the games. This passionate response to God's grandest promise is faith.

✠ ✠ ✠

It may seem a little forced to distinguish between God's promises and His offers; and I will not deny the charge if anyone chooses to bring it; but I make the distinction in order to emphasize the personal element in God's dealings with us. He comes nearer to us than even a promise brings Him: Person to person, He makes us offers.

His grand offer is His Son, whom He offers to the world as its Savior. This world is full of sin and misery, and it is in desperate need of someone to save it from these evils. Reformers and theorists are not wanting. The world is like an invalid with a disease of many years' standing, who has tried many physicians and spent much money on them, but is no better, but rather growing worse. Is there no balm in Gilead? Is there no physician there? God Himself comes to the rescue, and His remedy is nothing less than His own Son.

It is only expressing the same truth in another form if we say that Christ offers Himself to every person. When a person recognizes his or her identity as a sinner, condemned by justice and exposed to the loss of destiny, the value of the offer of a Savior is appreciated. But even one not so ripe for salvation as this might be awakened to the true position of affairs by the mere fact that a Savior is offered. As a person who has been in an accident, on awaking and seeing in the bedroom doctors, nurses, and weeping relatives, becomes aware that something serious has happened; so a thoughtful person, realizing that Christ is offering Himself as Savior, might well ask why such an offer is necessary. *The Son of God gave His life for me; but how did I stand in need of such a sacrifice?*

What have I done that I should require an atonement to be made for me at such price? What danger am I exposed to that the Son of God should have become incarnate to deliver me? Along such a line of reflection anyone might come to realize the value of Christ. Who does not acknowledge that the life and death of Christ form the mightiest event that ever happened in this world? *The Son of God incarnate! The Son of God dead upon the cross! What then is that to me? What am I getting out of it? Christ is not dead, He is living still. With all that history at His back, He comes to me and offers Himself as my Savior.* And, when my soul rises in humility and timid gratitude to accept the offer, feeling it to be the greatest chance I shall ever have in time or eternity, this is faith.

In this lecture I have been less desirous of giving an exact definition of faith than of commending it as an act or habit to cultivate; and, in conclusion, I should like, with the same end in view, to mention one form of faith that lends itself to easy cultivation. If any is unaware how to begin to exercise faith, the easiest form of it is prayer. This is a response to God's revelation of Himself; for the one who comes to God in prayer must believe that He is. It is a response to God's promises, for one of the principal arts of prayer is to plead the promises. And it is a response to God's offers: the best way of replying to Christ's offer of Himself is to speak to Him, and this is prayer. A single genuine prayer, and the life of faith is begun; and we have God's own word for it. "And everyone who calls on the name of the Lord will be saved" (Acts 2:21).

⚜HOPE⚜

Let us begin, as usual, with a word or two about the connection. The three Christian virtues—faith, hope, and love—are intimately connected. Faith belongs more to the intellectual, hope more to the will, and love more to the emotions. Faith is a vision of the spiritual and eternal world; hope is the effort of the will to secure the objects that faith reveals; love is the glow of desire for these objects, and sets the will in motion. In strict logic, love ought to be treated before hope, but we naturally reserve it for the last place, following the example of St. Paul, because it is the greatest.

Hope is with many people a matter of temperament. They have the temperament which is called *sanguineous.* They seem to see by nature the sunny side of things; they are always expecting success, and they rise like a cork from beneath the attempts of misfortune to depress them. The opposite temperament is the *melancholic.* As the name indicates, it is disposed to gloomy views, sees the seamy side of everything, and is always anticipating evil rather than good. As someone has wittily observed, if two people touch a bee, the one gets honey and the other gets stung; if two approach a bush, the one gathers a rose and the other is jagged with a thorn; if two people are gazing at the same quarter of the sky, the one remarks only the silver lining, the other only the black cloud.

Certainly it is a precious heritage to be born with a hopeful disposition. The one who, when it is midnight, remembers that the dawn is coming, and in the dead of winter has thoughts of the spring, is a wise person, and, in nine cases out of ten, events will justify that confidence, for the wheel of fortune turns round, and the part of it which is the bottom only requires half a revolution to be the top. The tide of opportunity rises at some time to everyone's feet, and the hopeful person is best prepared to take advantage of it.

Most people require a little bit of success to make them hopeful; a little encouragement, a little sunshine is all they need to cause all that is best in them to expand and to extract from them their best work. But there are those whose hopefulness is of such a buoyant order that they can go on hoping even when everything is against them, and obstacles and reverses appear actually to add to their good spirits. Such natures are invaluable to any cause; they carry a breeze with them wherever they go; the gloom passes from people's faces at the sight of them and is succeeded by smiles; discouraged adherents rally again, and the impossible becomes easy. It was attributed to the late Earl of Beaconsfield, as a quality invaluable to the party he led, that his hopes rose in proportion to the difficulties he had to encounter, and that he was never so brilliant as when his back was at the wall; but one sees in the condition of the opposite political party at the present hour how rare is the power of maintaining a spirit of cheerfulness and steadiness in the cold shade of opposition.

Temperament may be the source of hope; but its origin may be deeper, namely, principle, and this is better. This is the peculiar quality of Christian hope, which is not the perquisite of those endowed with a certain temperament, but may, on the contrary, be the attainment of those most disposed to melancholy; for the reason of it is not in themselves, but in Another.

When the attitude of the mind to the future is spoken of with reference not to the individual but to the race, we call it by more high-sounding names; the hopeful state of mind is called *optimism* and the reverse *pessimism*. Philosophers are generally understood to have risen superior to such frailties of human nature as temperament and to be able to contemplate truth with calm and unprejudiced eyes; but this supposed superiority may be an illusion, and the bias of natural disposition probably asserts itself in them as in other people. At all events, among thinkers there have always been optimists and pessimists. In the ancient world one sage was called the laughing philosopher and another the weeping philosopher, and these adjectives might be applied with equal propriety to rival schools of our own day.

> Pessimism feels in the marrow of its bones
> The heavy and the weary weight
> Of all this unintelligible world.

It dwells, with an excess of sensibility, on the fortuitous and destructive element in nature, on the earthquakes and storms by which the intelligence is baffled and chaos brought back again, on the immeasurable conflict in nature between the strong and the weak, in which the latter must go to the wall, and, above all, on the misery and aimlessness of human life, on the prevalence of disease and the inevitability of death, on the stupidity of the country and the depravity of the city, on man's inhumanity to man, and on his still more appalling cruelty to womanhood and childhood. It is the mood of Hamlet when, smarting under

> . . . The whips and scorns of time,
> The oppressor's wrong, the proud man's
>   contumely,
> The pangs of despised love, the law's delay,
> The insolence of office, and the spurns
> That patient merit of the unworthy takes,

He exclaimed—

> "O God, God,
> How weary, flat, stale, and unprofitable
> Seem to me all the uses of this world."

It is the mood of the Ecclesiast, as he moves from scene to scene of human life, but can find nothing new under the sun—nothing to relieve the monotony of existence—but declares that all is vanity and vexation of spirit.

In most minds pessimism is only a mood easily blown away by breezes of enjoyment or sturdy blasts of action;

but some have allowed it to harden till it becomes a doctrine and a creed. There is a philosophical pessimism that maintains that the evil in the world so far outweighs the good, and that it is so hopeless to expect any real improvement, that the rational destiny of the human race would be to disappear by a simultaneous act of suicide. One would naturally suppose such notions incompatible with religion; and, in fact, those who hold pessimistic opinions in doctrinaire form are usually unbelievers in an overruling Providence. But, strange to say, one of the most widely diffused religions of the world is thoroughly pessimistic in spirit. Buddhism looks upon human existence as evil in itself, and as so great an evil that the true ideal of humankind is relief from the burden of personal existence through reabsorption into the formless All out of which they came.

Optimism is the reverse of pessimism, and it is far more characteristic of the modern world. It is sometimes said that the golden age of the ancient world lay behind, whereas that of the modern world is in front. The golden age of the ancients was a scene of peace and plenty, produced without human aid and to be enjoyed without exertion; the golden age to which the modern person looks forward is to be the creation of human foresight and industry, and idleness will be excluded from the earthly paradise. Whatever it may be due to—whether to an instinct of the more energetic races, or to the wonderful improvements and progress witnessed in recent centuries—the belief is almost universal among the Western peoples that there is a good time coming, and that the course of humanity will continue upward and onward. Philosophy has sometimes tried to find in human nature a reason to justify this belief, but the great majority concur without any close inquiry into its grounds.

It is usually said that Christianity is optimistic. And this is true; but it might also be said that it is pessimistic. It does not believe in any inherent law of amelioration in this world. It views human nature as fallen and incapable of its own salvation. Left to themselves, people would grow worse, instead of better. But through this very pessimism Christianity is led to optimism because, despairing of humanity, it lays hold upon God, and it cleaves to Him with all the more tenacity the more conscious it is of the gulf into which it would fall without Him.

Thus by two pathways we have been led to the conclusion that hope for humankind is not in ourselves but out of ourselves. It is not subjective but objective. Of course, as a feeling, it is subjective, but that to which the feeling clings is not evolved out of our own interior, but presented from the outside: it descends from above; and hence its substantiality. A classical author says, "Hope is pursued by fear, and is the name of an uncertain good"; and this is profoundly true when it rests on nothing but temperament or sentiment. It is different, however, when what it clings to has a divine guarantee.

This Christian hope possesses. The objects to which it is directed are revealed in the Word of God. Thus, St. Paul says, "that through endurance and the encouragement of the Scriptures we might have hope" (Romans 15:4). In fact, God Himself is both the inspirer and the object of hope. Hence, He is called again and again in Scripture "the God of hope." So the Son of God is called "Christ our hope"; and in another place St. Paul denominates Him "Christ in you, the hope of glory." These are sufficient indications of the source whence Christian hope is derived and of what imparts to its stability. The feeling in our hearts may come and go, but the object outside remains the same yesterday, today, and forever. The more often we return to it, the more will doubts and fears fade away.

Whether it be the future of ourselves as individuals or the future of the world we are contemplating, it is equally true that Christ is our hope.

Consider, first, our own individual future. If our future is in our own hands or dependent only on other human beings, we must be in the greatest uncertainty about it, for who can tell what a day may bring forth? But, if it is out of our hands and in His, how safe it is, and how confident we may be about it! If He has begun a good work, He will complete it. As the arc of a circle, however fragmentary it may be, carries on the mind to the perfect whole, so Christ's work, though now imperfect, always looks onward, and contains the promise and the potency of perfection. Painful even as our depression on account of our failures may be, when we think of our lives as our own work, we have only to consider them as His workmanship, in order to be assured that our character will one day be without spot or wrinkle.

In the same way, when we think of the world at large—of its condition and prospects—there is overwhelming cause for sadness as long as we regard it as of our own making. But take in the fact that Christ has entered into human history and that He is controlling all events and guiding them to a foreordained issue, and then depression evaporates and we glory in the progress of the kingdom of God. The Father has given the kingdom to the Son, and the Son must reign till all enemies are put under His feet. Our little contribution which we call life is taken up into this whole and glorified in it. So is the work of the church, or the work of our generation. In itself it is trivial, but, in the place where He puts it, it is indispensable, for it is the link binding the past to the future. It is an arc of the circle of God's purpose and Christ's achievement; and the grandeur of the whole is in the fragment. I often think of the new consciousness of time Christianity imparts. A Christian thinks not only of what he or she is doing today, but of what that action will be doing a hundred or a thousand years hence.

Not only is Christ called our hope in Scripture, but the vitality of this virtue is specially connected with His resurrection according to St. Peter, God "has given us new birth into a living hope through the resurrection of Jesus Christ from the dead" (1 Peter 1:3). What is the reason for this? How does Christ's resurrection specially kindle hope? It does so because it is the most authentic glimpse ever afforded to humanity into the eternal world. The instinct of immortality is innate in humans; so much so that even pagans, like Cicero and Seneca, could argue for its trustworthiness from the fact of its universality; and other noble heathens, like Socrates and Plato, developed impressive arguments in support of the doctrine. It is a beautiful belief, and the best of human beings naturally incline to it. Yet in all ages, while so doing, men and women have been tormented with a doubt due to the fact that none ever actually came back from the other side of the gates of death. Why should not the gates of death be opened from within? Why should not one at least be allowed to appear—even for an hour—a representative person, worthy to be the mouthpiece of all the dead? Such is the irrepressible longing of the human heart; and the answer to it is the resurrection of Jesus from the dead. He was the representative person, worthy to appear and speak for all.

But the resurrection of Jesus is only like the claw of a prehistoric specimen, from which the skillful naturalist can construct the whole animal. If it be true, then immensely more is guaranteed. The life to come, in all its essential features, is rendered indubitable, and hope proceeds to fix its tentacles in it. In Scripture Christian hope is called by such names as "the hope of eternal life" and "the hope that is stored up for you in heaven." St. Peter, who has been called the apostle of hope (as St. Paul may be called the apostle of faith and St. John the apostle of love), speaks of "an inheritance that can never perish, spoil or fade—kept in heaven for you" (1 Peter 1:4). Undoubtedly, this future inheritance is the supreme, though not the exclusive, object of Christian hope; and in the apostolic age, at the commencement of Christianity, it laid extraordinary hold of the hearts of believers. So occupied were the early Christians with the inheritance they were about to enter, and the splendor of which threw all earthly possessions and prizes completely into the shade, that they were in danger of neglecting their homes and their business, and St. Paul and others had to urge them to think with more moderation on the subject. So eager were they not to be kept away from it that they not only willingly faced the persecution and martyrdom by which they would be carried more quickly there but even courted them; their preachers had to warn them against rushing at their own will upon death.

All this is changed now. The world is too much with us, and it is so real to our apprehension that the other world appears shadowy. The hope laid up in heaven does not captivate us much. Why is this? Perhaps it is because we take our profession of religion too easily; we are too afraid of giving offense; we provoke no opposition; we do not take up the cross and follow Jesus. The result is that we are comfortable and unmolested. But we pay the penalty of our comfort. Our spirits grow gross and vulgar, and our hope loses its intensity.

When Christians were sacrificing everything in this world for Christ, the world to come was exceedingly credible and delightful; and I have no doubt the day may come when, as Christians are persecuted for their faith, the hope of heaven will again be as great a power as ever.

It is a power when it is realized. It is no mere idle

expenditure of emotion on distant objects, having nothing to do with the present. To think often of heaven breeds heavenly-mindedness. They who intensely desire to be in heaven instinctively make themselves ready to go there, realizing that heaven is a prepared place for a prepared people. As St. John says, "Everyone who has this hope in him purifies himself, just as he is pure" (1 John 3:3). And St. Paul calls hope "an anchor for the soul." When the winds of passion are blowing and the billows of temptation rising and the darkness of doubt brooding, the soul is ready to drift on the hungry rocks; but the recollection of the immeasurable prize, to be won or lost in the hereafter, steadies it and enables it to avoid the danger till the day breaks and the shadows flee away.

❧LOVE❧

Professor Drummond entitled his little book on love *The Greatest Thing in the World*, and the vast circulation which it secured in every part of the globe proved how the suggestion had appealed to the general mind. But he was only following the hint given in the saying of St. Paul, "but the greatest of these is love" (1 Corinthians 13:13). And St. Paul was only following in the wake of Jesus who, when asked, "Which is the greatest commandment in the Law?" replied "'Love the Lord your God with all your heart and with all your soul and with all your mind.' This is the first and greatest commandment. And the second is like it: 'Love your neighbor as yourself'" (Matthew 22:36-39).

The belief that love is the greatest thing in the world may be called a growing conviction; the more mature the mind of humankind becomes, the clearer is its verdict to this effect; and this is the judgment of those most entitled to express an opinion. Inferior minds have, indeed, different ideals; and in earlier ages other qualities were placed far before love. Thus, strength long had its worshipers, and it will always have them among the immature and unreflecting, who bow the knee to physical development and material resources. At a more advanced stage, cleverness was considered the greatest thing in the world, and there are still multitudes who testify unbounded admiration for the intellectual force that can crush an adversary or the adroitness that can circumvent him. But, while the notoriety of the hour may rise loud round those distinguished for strength and cleverness, it is found, when the clamor subsides, that the abiding homage of the human heart can be given only to those who have served their circle or their generation with the ministry of love. "Love never fails."

It is one of the most signal evidences of the goodness of the Author of our existence that in the scheme of providence there is provision made, between the cradle and the grave, for the supply of the individual of many different kinds of love in succession, while the heart, on its part, puts forth one new blossom after another to the very end. We open our baby eyes on love, with which we have been already surrounded before we were able to appreciate it—the love of parents. Then, as the family fills, and its connections multiply, we are enriched with the love of brothers and sisters, cousins and other relatives. When we emerge from childhood into that period of life when the currents of the heart are most copious, we begin to experience the love of country and of comradeship; friendship springs up with those of the same sex, and a still dearer tie with the opposite sex. This tie finds its consummation in marriage; and then follows the love of offspring with its manifold lights and shades of joy and pride, anxiety and sorrow. To some it is vouchsafed to experience the love of grandparents for grandchildren; and, at even a later stage, a fresh bud may burst on the old tree in the love of great-grandparents for great-grandchildren.

Even these are not all the kinds of affection of which the heart is capable; but these are enough to show that under the one name of love many feelings are included, which really differ widely from one another. The love, for example, of those of the same sex is exceedingly different from that of persons of opposite sexes, and a person who has experienced the one may have very little idea what the other is like. One or more kinds of affection may be omitted in the development of a human heart through no fault of its own, but through the appointment of God; and such an omission may not prejudice the growth of an affectionate nature; but the heart cannot miss any of its legitimate opportunities without suffering loss. As a rule, those are happiest whose development has been most normal—the heart unfolding each new blossom as the season for it arrives, and every kind of affection being experienced in full measure. It is sad for a child whose parents are alive never to have received in its fullness the love of father or mother, or never to have given love back in return. It is a kind of mutilation and must leave the whole nature permanently impoverished. If any kind of love is denied to us, it is well to make up for the loss by loving more amply in some other direction. For example, one who has no brothers or sisters should have all the wider a circle of friends.

Professor Drummond, in another of his books, *The Ascent of Man*, has written with great beauty on mater-

nal love, which he evidently regarded as the choicest
flower and blossom of earthly affection. He traced its history down through the dim eons of prehistoric times,
from the jealous instinct of brute mothers to its most perfect refinement in the womanhood of the Christian world.
He showed that this instinct for the preservation of life of
others had been the great counterpoise to the instinct of
self-preservation. Thus from immemorial ages there has
been woven into the web of the world's history not a single but a double thread—not only the struggle for existence, often degenerating into cruelty and violence, but
the struggle for the existence of others, marked all along
its course by self-sacrifice. And so it has come to pass that
the world has been not merely a field of battle and butch-
ery but a scene of heroism and ever-waxing beauty.
Whether or not we accept the assumption that maternal
love of today is a development that has grown from millennium to millennium, till it has reached its present
depth and tenderness, at any rate no one who has enjoyed
the privilege of watching it at close quarters—its purity,
its passion, its cooing happiness and elation, the power it
imparts to the mother of overcoming sleep and rendering
with cheerfulness and dignity the most menial services—
will fail to bend before it in lowly worship and acknowledge that, if there is one divine thing in this world, it is a
mother's love.

But even those kinds of affection that have been less
celebrated have their honor and value. The love, for
instance, of brother and sister may be of exquisite tenderness, as it may be of priceless profit to both parties,

when he, the stronger, learns gentleness by stooping to
her weakness, and she, the weaker, acquires courage
and strength in the effort to keep step with his career.
There are few figures more touching in human life than
such a sister as Dorothy Wordsworth, the companion of
one engaged in achieving a difficult and noble life-work
in the eyes of the world, which she is furthering all the
time with the ministry of frugality, practicality, and good
sense, content to remain invisible in the background,
her unselfish heart satisfied with the honors that are
falling upon him.

The love of friends has had ample justice done to it
from the time of David and Jonathan down to our own
time, when Lord Tennyson has — in *In Memoriam* — raised
to his friend, Arthur Henry Hallam, a monument more
enduring than brass. In this poem we see what friendship
can do to quicken anyone's best powers and to develop all
that is noble in character; for a superior friend's gener-
ous expectations are a standard to which one's own
achievements must strive to rise, while, if the friend's
character is of the right stamp, his or her presence serves
as a second conscience, administering the requisite check
when one's own conscience is for the moment remiss, and
forming a tribunal before which one cannot appear with
a base purpose.

Of course, however, it is love between man and
woman which is love *par excellence*. It is this that poets
speak of as the one experience which, if obtained and
held, makes life a success, but, if missed, makes all a
blank —

For life, with all it yields of joy and woe,
Of hope and fear,
Is just our chance o' the prize of learning love.

In works of imagination love occupies the same place as Christ does in sermons: It is the element on which the savor of the whole depends.

In sober fact, this is in many respects, the greatest thing in the world. Never is a human heart purer — purer from selfishness and purer from animal desire — than when it falls honestly and thoroughly in love. Nothing marks a more decided and undeniable advance in civilization than an improvement in the mode of conceiving what love is and in the modes of carrying on the relationship — such as can be noted, for example, in a comparison of the eighteenth and the nineteenth centuries. Nothing is such a spur to the exertion of all one's powers as the desire to provide for the fruition of love; and a pure love, housed in a happy home, is, next to the grace of God, the best blessing anyone can win.

Though, up to this point, I have been speaking of many kinds of love, these have all been between people. Is there no other of which the heart is capable, and for which it is destined? Yes; there are objects of love for the human heart both below and above other people.

Of the objects beneath people much need not be said; but I will not miss the opportunity of remarking in passing that the affection of the Arab for his steed, of the

Indian for his elephant, of the shepherd for his dog, is a sentiment creditable to human nature. The treatment of the lower animals is one of the most accurate measurements of the stage which civilization has reached in any country. Cruelty to these dumb companions of humanity's earthly lot hardens the heart and coarsens the character; and few movements can be more acceptable to the Creator, who pours out His love on even the humblest of His creatures, than the societies formed in our day for promoting kindness toward the lower animals.

But it is of love at the opposite end of the scale I wish to speak—love to beings above others.

Even so wise a representative of the ancient world as Aristotle says, "There is no such thing as love to God; it is absurd to speak of anything of the kind; for God is an unknowable being." It is impossible to conceive words that could bring out more clearly the contrast between the circle of thought within which the ancient world moved and that wherein those move who have obtained their notions of the universe from the Bible. Even in the Old Testament God is a being who loves, and loves intensely. "As a father has compassion on his children, so the LORD has compassion on those who fear him" (Psalm 103:13). "Can a mother forget the baby at her breast and have no compassion on the child she has borne? Though she may forget, I will not forget you!" (Isaiah 49:15). "I have loved you with an everlasting love; I have drawn you with loving-kindness" (Jeremiah 31:3). "I will betroth you to me forever; I will betroth you in righteousness and justice, in love and compassion. I will betroth you in faithfulness, and you will acknowledge the LORD" (Hosea 2:19-20). In the New Testament the revelation of the love of God is carried much further, till it culminates in the incomparable saying, "God is love."

It is often said that any modern child acquainted with the rudiments of science stands on a far higher level than Aristotle, though he was the most scientific head in the ancient world, so far have the discoveries of modern times left the ancient world behind; and it is just as true to say that any modern child acquainted with the Bible stands high above Aristotle in the knowledge of God. To Aristotle God was, according to the sage's own admission, an unknown being; but to those who have the Bible in their hands He is a being known to be living and infinitely loving; and this renders possible the budding of the noblest blossom of the heart—the love of God. Just as a human heart is born with the kinds of love already discussed— love to parents, love to friends, love to children, and so on—potential in it, waiting only for time and opportunity to burst and develop, so every heart is born with the capacity of loving God; and this must, in the nature of the case, be the highest and most influential of all such capabilities. But the sunshine which opens the bud, causing the potentiality to become actuality, is the love of God revealed and realized. So St. John explained its philosophy—"We love because he first loved us" (1 John 4:19).

I was much struck by this testimony of someone as to his own experience: "All that I ever heard—and I heard much—about the love of God was to me sound and smoke, until I realized that the Son of God had given up

His life on the cross to redeem me from my sins." And there is no doubt that this is the way in which most people begin to love God, if they love Him with reality and with intensity. It is not only that the love of the Father is supremely and finally revealed in the gift of His Son; but in Christ Himself the divine love shines forth in the most affecting and attractive of all forms; it shines out all along the course of His life with increasing brightness; and it blazes from His cross. We, therefore, love Jesus first, and then the Father—we come to the Father through the Son.

There can be no doubt that, ever since He was crucified on Calvary, Jesus Christ has commanded the love of tens of thousands in every generation, and that the strength of Christianity at any time is accurately measured by the number of those who love Him, and the intensity with which they do so. If the question be asked, "What is a Christian?", many answers could doubtless be given; but none is more to the point than this: "A Christian is one who loves Christ."

Sometimes this love dawns upon the heart with sudden rapture, similar to that which, in the relations of human beings, often accompanies what is called falling in love. But this sublime happiness is not vouchsafed to all. Many who undoubtedly love Him have no recollection when they commenced to do so. The essential question is not, however, how love began, but whether it is *growing*. And love of Christ grows exactly by the same means as love of anyone else—by being constantly in His company, by speaking often to Him, by gazing on the beauty of His character, and by not forgetting all His benefits.

✢ ✢ ✢

Some are jealous of expressions of love to God because they suspect that these may be substituted for acts of love to others. And it cannot be denied that zeal for God has sometimes been associated with cruelty and hardheartedness toward others, as, for example, in the burning of heretics and the torture of witches.

But such cases are exceptional and unnatural. The normal effect of love of God is love of others. Professor Drummond has drawn attention to the fact that the correct translation of a verse quoted already is not, "We love him because he first loved us," but "We love because he first loved us." The love of God realized leads to all kinds of love because it breaks down the natural selfishness of the heart which is the great obstacle to every kind of tender feeling toward others. Is it not a contradiction in terms to speak of loving Christ when we do not love our fellow human beings? If the word of Jesus has any weight with us, if His example, in any degree, influences our conduct, if His spirit has even faintly entered our heart, then we cannot be loveless to our fellow creatures. "And he has given us this command: Whoever loves God must also love his brother" (1 John 4:21).

In spite of the satire so frequently poured from the pulpit and through the press on the behavior of Christians to one another, the fact is, the feeling of true Christians for one another is very deep and tender. Let them meet anywhere—even in the ends of the earth—and recognize one another as such, and their hearts leap together at once, and there is nothing they will not do for one another. If they hesitate to give such recognition, it is because they are not sure of their ground; but let them be sure, and kindness follows immediately.

I venture even to say that the average behavior of Christians to those whom they cannot identify as real Christians proves that the love of God in their hearts has improved their feelings and their conduct. It is, indeed, impossible to feel for such the same love as for those who are brethren in the Lord. But all people are potential Christians; they are all capable of being saved and becoming heirs of immortality and this gives them all a claim on our love — not only on our evangelistic and proselytizing zeal, but on our humanity and kindness. On this subject, let me quote a few words from the same author with whom I commenced this chapter. Addressing a band of missionaries, Professor Drummond once said:

> You can take nothing greater to the heathen world than the impress and reflection of the love of God upon your own character. This is the universal language. It will take you years to speak in Chinese or in the dialects of India. But, from the day you land, that language of love, understood by all, will be pouring forth its unconscious eloquence. Take into your new sphere of labor, where you also mean to lay down your life, that simple charm, and your lifework must succeed. You can take nothing greater, you can take nothing less. You may take every accomplishment, you may be

braced for every sacrifice, but, if you give your body to be burned and have not love, it will profit you and the cause of Christ nothing.

ABOUT THE AUTHOR

JAMES STALKER (1848–1927) was born in Scotland and was a minister, scholar, and writer. He served as professor of church history in the United Free Church College in Aberdeen from 1902 to 1926. He was well known as a visiting lecturer and spoke at many American colleges and seminaries. He was the author of several books, including *The Life of Saint Paul*, *The Life of Jesus Christ*, and *The Two St. Johns of the New Testament*.